MW01640163

Pout or Purpose?

A Simple Approach for Understanding Your *Purpose Pie* and Improving Your Life

---

By Harold Kerr, M.B.A.

Illustrations by Jay Mazhar
Edited by Lisa J. Voss

Published by:

For information, or to order books, contact:

K.C. Fox Publishing
P.O. Box 5446
Takoma Park, MD 20913
Email: publisher@kcfoxpublishing.com

Publisher's Cataloging-In-Publication Data
(Prepared by The Donohue Group, Inc.)

Kerr, Harold E., 1968-
Pout or purpose? : a simple approach for understanding your purpose pie and improving your life / by Harold Kerr ; illustrations by Jay Mazhar ; edited by Lisa J. Voss.
p. : ill. ; cm.
ISBN: 0-9767078-0-2
1. Self-actualization (Psychology) 2. Animals--Symbolic aspects. I. Mazhar, Jay. II. Voss, Lisa J. III. Title.
BF637.S4 K47 2005
158.1

Printed in the United States of America

Illustrations by Jay Mazhar
Edited by Lisa J. Voss

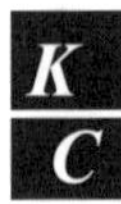

This book is dedicated in memory of Veronica Smith:
Who passed away early, but embodied the principles in the book.

Also to Krystalle Campo:
Who inspired me to finally write this book and helped me translate my vision onto paper.

Contents

Preface

Everything should be made as simple as possible...
—Albert Einstein

I'm a professional management consultant. I've spent my entire professional career helping companies and government entities improve their organizations. As the punch line of the joke below shows, consultants are not always that admired:

"Clearly, you're a consultant," says the shepherd.
"Correct," says the consultant as he loads his newly acquired "sheep" in his car. "But, how did you guess that?"
"No guessing required," answers the shepherd. "You showed up here although nobody called you. You wanted to get paid for an answer I already knew, to a question I never asked, and you don't know anything about my business. Now give me back my dog!"

—Author Unknown

While many of my fellow consultants and I will argue that we do provide value to the organizations we assist, my job began to wear on me—no matter how hard I worked, I was never fulfilled, nor did I feel like what I was doing with my life had any purpose. Ironically, large corporations and organizations paid me to improve their complex operations and problems, but I wasn't improving something as important as my own life.

During the winter of 2003, something happened that gave me a new perspective. A major snowstorm hit the East Coast and hospitals put out a call for people who owned four-wheel drive vehicles. I volunteered, and for two days, I drove people to and from the hospital: the radiology technician who had to perform an emergency ultrasound for a woman with a high-risk pregnancy; numerous nurses who had to perform their patient rounds; and after midnight on the second night, a rough-looking young man who was upset that he was not allowed to stay with his wife who had just given birth. He got more upset when none of the drivers volunteered to take him home because where he lived was "out of their way" (he lived in a bad neighborhood).

I somewhat reluctantly volunteered to take him home, and during the ride, I realized that one cannot always judge a book by its cover. The young man spoke with tears in his eyes about how proud he was about the birth of his child, and when I dropped him off, he told me to wait in the car while he went and got something. For a quick moment, I thought about the neighborhood I was in, and what he might be "getting." I was pleasantly surprised when he came out and gave me a gift for giving him a ride. Driving home, I realized that I received more satisfaction during those two days than I had in my 13-year consulting career working on multimillion-dollar projects.

Based on this experience, I realized my life needed change. I thought: If organizations paid me to fix their problems, then I should be able to fix my own problems! So I did what any good consultant would do: I developed a methodology to help me identify my purpose. Wait, it gets better. I then developed a model that divides almost everything in our lives into four—that's right, just four—aspects. Then, to obtain quantitative data, I developed a questionnaire that I could use to assess my life in the four areas. Before you dismiss this approach, let me tell you the results: (1) This book, and (2) The sense that my life has a purpose.

In sum, I realized that I receive satisfaction assisting people. So, I decided to help as many individuals as possible improve their lives by giving them a simple, yet comprehensive, method for doing so. *A consultant developing something simple?* I know that sounds like another joke, but I developed the following approach for understanding how to gain purpose in one's life:

Simple Approach

Task	Book Chapter
1. Understand the four major Life Aspects and the corresponding 25 Life Improvement Principles.	Chapters 2-5
2. Conduct an assessment: understand what's important; where you're satisfied; and where improvement is needed.	Chapter 6
3. Write a Purpose Statement.	Chapter 7
4. Develop a Life Improvement Action Plan.	Chapter 8

A few of my friends who read draft versions of the book stated (a little disappointedly!) that the 25 Life Improvement Principles presented in Chapters 2-5 were pretty simple and everyone should already know them. My reply was, "Exactly!" The principles are simple because life improvement can (and should) be simple, and not a long, drawn-out process that takes an inordinate effort. Interestingly, even though the principles are simple, when I asked my friends how often they followed the principles, and if they knew where they need the most improvement regarding these principles, more often than not, they sheepishly responded, "Not really."

To make the approach palatable, instead of writing the book in the dry prose typical to my consulting reports, I decided to write the book in a very simple (there's that word again) style. With help from my good friend Krystalle Campo, who's beginning her career writing creative stories, I used a story-telling style—a style of writing very effective for conveying messages—from Aesop's fables, to books popular in today's workplace, like the successful book *Who Moved My Cheese?* By telling a story, the approach comes to life.

At the end of each chapter, I switch back to real-life and present two sections that hopefully you'll find useful. First, I present a summary of the key points from the story, and second, I present a section entitled "Reader Reflection," where you are asked to relate the elements in the story to your own life. Included in this section are also some assignments for you to complete.

Based on the nature of the two sections at the end of each chapter, I suggest you take some time (a couple of minutes, or a couple of days) to think about what you've read, and to complete the assignments, before moving on to the next chapter. Also, consider going through these sections in a group, e.g., discuss them in a book club meeting.

Now, sit back and enjoy reading how the crafty consultant, Fixity Fox, helps his client, Pouting Pig, find his purpose.

Chapter 1: All Cooped Up!

A Pig, frustrated with his life, sits and cries.
A Fox, out for himself, the Pig befriends.
An offer of assistance is made;
And with that, a journey begins.

By the dawning light, a rather large Fox is seen walking through the woods on a quest for a meal. His long, red tail twitches to and fro as the smell of hens roosting on a nearby farm grows stronger. With each inhalation, the appetent Fox creates a menu for the week ahead: "Warm Wings on Wednesday, Tender Thighs on Thursday, Fried Feet on Friday. Sss… Saa… Arghhh! What am I to eat on Saturday?" Being a stickler for such things, Fox stops and contemplates a change in menu, but seeing that fowl is a favorite, he thinks hard to identify a Saturday meal. "Ah yes, Sautéed Scraps on Saturday."

Thoughts of feasting quicken this vulpine visitor's movement to the copious chicken coop—or, as Fox puts it, "a guaranteed meal." A guaranteed meal usually, but today, Fox is in for a surprise, not a treat.

Meanwhile, at the farm, a despondent Pig hides in the chicken coop crying, "I will never go back to the pig pen! Never! No one appreciates me, and nothing ever goes right for me. I don't know what to do with my life! I am nothing but a pouting Pig with problems!"

Unaware of Pig's presence, Fox presses forward, salivating toward the coop. A chicken near the door of the coop sees Fox approaching and clucks a warning to the other hens. "Fox is near! Beware!" The hen's cackling alarms the other hens, who begin scurrying around the coop for yet another fateful day of hide-or-be-a-treat.

Saturated in self-pity, Pig raises his head to the screams and scuffles of the hens, "Why do you run away from me? I don't want to be a bother, really. Should I leave? But, ohhhh, where would I go? If only I wasn't so useless. I'm a failure—I'm not fat enough, strong enough, smart enough. Woe is me!"

At the door of the coop arrives the Fox who, upon hearing the crying Pig, barks: "Silence, swine! Do you want to alert the farmer?"

"I'm-m-m sowwy," stammers Pig, "It's just that I have all these problems, and I—"

Ignoring Pig, Fox heads straight for a plump hen hiding behind a feeder. All of a sudden, Pig lets out a new round of crying, stopping Fox in his tracks. "What is it now swine?" Fox asks. "Can't you shut up?"

"You can't make me!" Pig squeals.

"Oh yeah?" Fox snarls, and with a twitch of his tail, he turns and pounces forward to pin the little runt to the ground. "I'll show you—you senseless thing." Seeing that Fox is about to attack, Pig squeals louder, causing Fox to lose concentration and miss his target, landing in a pile of hay next to Pig, who peeps out of the haystack with drooping eyes and a sniffling snout.

Shaking the hay off his well-groomed fur, Fox mumbles beneath his breath, "I'll never get a meal like this. There must be a better way to quiet this shoat. Hmmm, let's see. I can scare it—no, not that squealing swine. Eat it? Not exactly my taste." Fox, becoming more and more aggravated, thinks even harder, "I'll fix that, that—that's it! I'll fix the swine's problems. Fix the swine so I can dine. Ha, ha! Away from the hens is a Pig in his pen. Oh, how I like the sound of that." Fox, feeling quite clever, merrily whistles about his plan for Pig.

Hearing Fox, Pig turns his head and begins chortling at the whistling Fox. Fox grabs this opportunity to befriend Pig, "A smiling swine, how divine. So, you must be ready to leave?"

Pig, now aware of his smile, frowns and whines, "I can't go back out there."

"Oh?" And why is that?"

"I can't tell you. You won't understand."

"Alright then, be a snout with a pout!" Fox says as he pretends to leave the coop.

"I HAVE NO PURPOSE!"

Wails Pig, hoping Fox wouldn't leave.

Fox turns back and says, "Oh, you have no purpose, do you? Surely you're not serving any purpose in here. Coops are for chickens; not for other farm animals that happen to be having a bad hair day."

"But, but… I have problems!" Pig whimpers.

"Problems? Who doesn't have problems?" retorts Fox. "For example, take the cows out there in the pasture—there's a rumor going around that they've all gone stark-raving mad, but do you see them hiding in here with the chickens? No, they're out in the pasture where they belong, serving their purpose. So what problems do you have that could be so bad?"

Pig replies, "Everyone in my family is good at something but me. My father is president of the Porker's Compensation Commission. My mother heads up the local chapter of the woman's organization SOW. My sister won the blue ribbon at the spring fair yesterday for being the smartest pig in the county, and my brother is the best pig on the farm at finding truffles for the farmer to sell. My brother and sister told me this morning that because I don't do anything, I'm useless and don't have a purpose. That's why I'm never going back to the pen!"

"You mean you're in here squealing like a stuck pig for that?" Fox asks, annoyed. "What you mention is very easy to fix! If you come with me, I'll show you that all animals on this farm have a purpose—even a little runt like yourself!"

Pig lifts his head, and asks, "Do you have a purpose?"

Fox, never having thought about his purpose, puffs his chest, flips his tail, and states, "Of course I have a purpose. But, when you look as good as I do, you don't necessarily need one. Now, enough with the questions! I know exactly where a pig's purpose can be found."

Pig, happy for the attention, follows Fox out of the coop. Once outside, Fox charges toward Pig who screams, "Please, don't eat me!"

"Caught ya!" Fox exclaims as he snatches up a lost little chick from near Pig's hooves. "Silly swine, Foxes don't eat pork." Looking at his captive, Fox licks his lips and says inaudibly, "I prefer the other white meat."

But just as Fox is about to gobble up the little chick, Fox turns toward the terrified Pig, and remembering his grand plan, pats the chick on the head and releases it into the coop mumbling, "I'll catch you later." Fox faces Pig and says, "Besides, I would never eat a comrade. We shall serve each other, but not on a tray." They both watch the little chick scramble off. "Pig, I am here to help, and in return, I only ask two small favors."

"Anything, anything," responds Pig.

"First, you have to promise me that you will stay out of the chicken coop, never to return."

"But the chick—"

"No 'buts,' Pig! Secondly, if ever I am in the coop, you know, chatting with my feathered friends, and you see the farmer coming, you must grunt, grunt as loud as you can. You see, the farmer wishes to adorn his hideous wife with my beautiful fur."

"That's horrible!"

"Yes, Pig, it is. Now promise you will do that for me."

"I promise," says Pig sitting back on his bottom, clapping his hooves in excitement.

"Splendid, I am now your **Life Improvement Consultant**, and you are my client. I'm an expert at fixing problems, so call me Mr. Fixity Fox or Mr. Fox. And what shall I call you?"

"Wow, a 'client'! I've never been a client before!"

"Your name!" Fixity Fox barks.

"Oh, right! POUTING PIG! Everyone calls me Pouting Pig."

"Not necessarily a name to be proud of, but it will do. Now, Pork Chop-Chop! Time is of the essence. To my den! I mean, my office," orders Fixity Fox as he thinks to himself, "The sooner I placate this pesky Pig, the sooner I can begin marinating some nice-n-plump chicken that would make a certain Kentucky Colonel proud."

Pouting Pig springs up and follows Fixity Fox back to his office. Once there, Fixity Fox turns to Pouting Pig and says, "You wait outside while I get my consulting material. Meanwhile, I want you to write a list in the dirt of all that ails you."

"Ails me? What does that mean?"

"Write a list of what you were blabbering about back there in the coop." Fixity Fox turns away from Pouting Pig and goes into his den.

Once inside, Fixity Fox paces back and forth in his library searching for something, anything, he can use to help Pouting Pig. "Think, Fox, think!" Finally, sitting at his desk, Fixity Fox turns on his computer and opens his ***Foxfire*** web browser and enters, "How to Solve a Pig's Problems," and with a click of the mouse, thousands of answers to the query appear, including, of course, the occasional sordid listing:

527,437 Web Results Found:

1. No Longer Afraid: Memoirs of the Three Little… "No,"
2. Stammer No More: A Porky P… "No,"
3. This Little Piggy Got Some: A Lonely Pig Dating Service "Hmmm… This is interesting… No, NO!"

Fixity Fox scrolls down the page, opening and closing a list of seemingly endless web pages. Finally, he sees something promising from the Crafty Consultant Website:

420. Out Fox 'em Every Time! Crafty Consultant Tips to Fix Any Problem

Fixity Fox browses a summary of the result:

*How consultants can solve **any** client's problems:*
Do some quick research, create an approach with fancy graphics, use impressive sounding consultant terms, talk to some experts (the ones who really know the answers), take credit, and fake the rest!

"This is exactly what I need to make me smart! Well, smarter than I already am," exclaims Fixity Fox as he prints the numerous results from the site. Happy with his research, he grabs the results from his printer, jots down some notes, sketches some diagrams, and remembers to bookmark the Lonely Pig Dating Service website—just in case.

Armed with newfound knowledge, and smartly dressed in a tweed blazer with the name "Fixity Fox" taped on the lapel, he emerges from his den and walks over to Pouting Pig, who has fallen asleep.

"Wake up, Pig! Did you do what I asked you to do?"

"Yes, I wrote my list," replies a groggy Pouting Pig who points on the ground.

Fixity Fox looks in the dirt and reads Pouting Pig's list out loud:

Pouting Pig's List

- Nobody likes me - I'm useless - I'll never amount to anything - I'm too thin for a Pig - I'm not smart - I feel so empty inside

"That's quite a list. Some of which comes as no surprise—you being a pouter and all," says Fixity Fox as he scribbles the list on a sheet of paper, stuffs it into his pocket and then consults his research: Consultant Tip #7: *Create an approach with a fancy name.*

"I have designed a **Life Improvement Methodology** just for you."

"A metha . . . what?" Pouting Pig asks.

"A methodology—an approach. Pay attention, and in just four easy steps, you'll be a pouter no more." Fixity Fox presents Pig with a graphic from the Crafty Consultant website:

Life Improvement Methodology

"Now listen carefully," says Fixity Fox, glancing at his research. "The first step of your *uniquely tailored* methodology involves understanding the different Life Aspects. Once you have an acute understanding of these, we'll then conduct an assessment, and based on the assessment, you'll undergo a paradigm shift and write a purpose statement, which will be followed by us brainstorming and thinking out-of-the-box to create an action plan."

Fixity Fox catches his breath and continues, "So, now that we clearly understand what we're about to accomplish, do you have any questions?"

A stunned Pouting Pig looks at Fixity Fox and says, "Fixity Fox—"

"It's *Mr.* Fixity Fox, or Mr. Fox!" admonishes Fixity Fox.

Pouting Pig responds meekly, "Mr. Fixity Fox, you went through that really fast. I didn't understand everything you said."

"Excellent! The methodology wouldn't be as powerful if clients totally understood it. Besides, everything will fall into place as I take you through the process. So, just be a good client and try to keep up. To begin Step 1 of our methodology, let me show you the key aspects of all our lives—almost everything we do, or that is important to us, can be illustrated in a model grouped into four Life Aspects."

Life Aspects Model

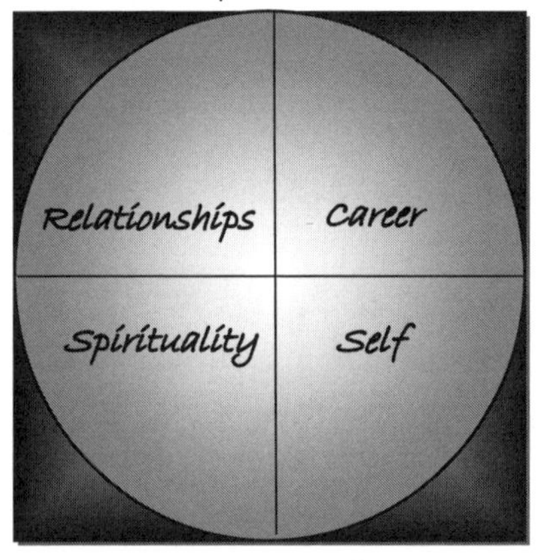

"It looks like a big pie!" Pouting Pig shouts as he licks his snout.

"It is ***not*** a pie! It's a scientifically developed model. And to show you how this model relates to you, just think about it, Pig. You say no one likes you—guess what? You have a ***relationship*** problem. Maybe it's all that whining you do. And just look at your ***self***; you're a mess. Oh, and let's not forget the 'woe, is me, I feel so empty' drivel. There's reason for your emptiness, and it has to do with your lack of ***spirituality***. And you wouldn't be so useless if you weren't hiding in the hen house. Find a ***career***!" Fox scolds.

Fixity Fox looks at the sulking Pouting Pig and lets his words sink in before continuing. "But there *is* hope for you Pig. To identify your purpose, you first have to identify how important each Life Aspect is to you, because it's from these aspects your purpose is derived. Then, you assess how satisfied, or in your case, dissatisfied, you are with your life in each of the Life Aspects. And based on the combination of your importance and satisfaction with the Life Aspects, improvement areas can be identified; with the final goal being to identify specific improvement actions to prioritize."

"Pri-or-ri-tize?" Pouting Pig stammers.

To which Fixity Fox crisply responds, "Yes. Prioritize! A wonderful word for a Pig whose problems leave him pained. Prioritizing makes your insane life sane."

"I surely do like the sound of that, Mr. Fox," exclaims Pouting Pig. "You're so clever!"

"Yes I am. And you're in good hands. I've successfully done this many times before."

"You have?"

"What—you think you're the first pig I've fixed? Why else would they call me Fixity Fox? Now here, take this pen and paper. I want you to write down everything you learn." Referring to his consultant tips, Fixity Fox continues, "To learn a bit more about each of the four Life Aspects, which is *Step 1* of our methodology, we have some farm animals to visit—Field Experts of sorts."

Life Improvement Methodology

And with that, the naïve Pouting Pig follows the tricky Fixity Fox back to the farm, along a path that will change both of their lives forever.

Fixity Fox's Introduction Material

- Everyone has problems, but don't let them get in the way of your purpose!
- To identify your purpose:
  - ~ Step 1: Understand the *Life Aspects*.
  - ~ Step 2: Conduct an assessment:
    - Determine what's important to you.
    - Determine how satisfied you are.
    - Identify and prioritize improvement areas.
  - ~ Step 3: Write your Purpose Statement.
  - ~ Step 4: Develop an Improvement Plan.

Reader Reflection:

I'll start off with the $64,0000 question: What's your purpose in life? Do you have one? It's important to note that everyone's purpose is different. Some are grand "change the world" purposes; others are more personal and intimate such as "raising a loving family" or "helping others." No one purpose is better than another.

Take a moment to think about your purpose. **Assignment 1:** Write your purpose down on a piece of paper. (You can have more than one.) C'mon on now, you're not writing!

Okay, for those of you that followed instructions, was it difficult for you to write down your purpose? If so, why do you think it was?

I want you now to think about the problems in your life. What things are keeping you from achieving your purpose in life? Even if you're not a pouter like our friend Pouting Pig, everyone has something they would place on their problems list. **Assignment 2:** Take a few moments to jot down your list of problems. (You don't need to draw it in the dirt like Pouting Pig—a piece of paper will be fine!)

Now look at your list. Are you able to discern which problems are the really important problems; which ones are impediments to achieving your purpose in life; and which ones are simply distractions that don't warrant much attention? The main purpose of this book is to help you make this assessment by identifying what's truly important to you to give your life purpose.

Lastly, what have you done in the past to address the important problems? What approach have you taken? Who have you enlisted to help you? The rest of the book will help answer these questions. (Keep your written purpose and problems list handy for later!)

When you're ready, on to the first Life Aspect—**Relationships**.

Chapter 2: Life Aspect—Relationships

There are many around us, each with different roles in our lives:
Friends, sisters, brothers, fathers and mothers.
While going it alone is a noble thing,
We all recognize we need relationships with others.

Back at the farm, a Labrador Retriever drinks from her water dish. Before the farmer and his family left for the fair, he told Lovable Lab to take care of the farm. The farm is large, making this no easy job; but at the end of the day, Lovable Lab knows she will be rewarded with a treat. This farm is her home, and every animal on the farm is a member of her family. Lovable Lab enjoys protecting her family from danger, so once done drinking, she begins her morning rounds.

About this time, Fixity Fox, and Pouting Pig stumbling along behind him, reach the farm. Fixity Fox is unsure where to begin Pouting Pig's journey to find his purpose. He takes Pouting Pig's list of problems out of his jacket pocket and reads it to himself. He then crumples the list into a ball and puts it back into his pocket thinking, "What a helpless sap! What's the quickest way I can convince Pig that his problems are solved so I can dump this slow swine and be on my merry way? Maybe I could pay another Piglet to pretend that she's enamored with him." Fox begins to chuckle as he remembers the *Lonely Pig Dating Service* website, "With a little bit of that, Pouting Pig will be fixed for life! Heck, we can just go back to my den, and I can post a personal ad!"

"Hey Pig, what do you think about this for a solution: SWP (Single Whiney Pig) seeks a lifetime pen-pal that will keep me far away from the chicks." Fixity Fox turns to face Pouting Pig, only to notice the little Pig aimlessly circling himself. "Hey Pig! Pig! What the heck are you doing?"

"I'm … arggg… this thing … it just won't stay still!"

"What thing?"

This thing… weeee, weee … let me at it, let me at …"

"You mean your tail?"

"Yeah, my tai... my… Oohhhh…" Pouting Pig stops, and topples over, muttering.

Disgusted by Pouting Pig's silly antics, Fixity Fox decides he's had quite enough—he is much too sophisticated to be helping this hopeless pouter. Fixity Fox calculates that if he left Pouting Pig now, he would have enough time to run into the henhouse and capture a five-piece before Pouting Pig ever reached the farm. Deciding that this was the best course of action for a self-respecting fox like himself, Fixity Fox picks up his pace and trots toward the chicken coop.

As the sight of the promised land comes into view, Fixity Fox hears faint barking coming in his direction. "Blasted!" He mutters, as he stops and considers his next move. "Not another encounter with the Lab! If she catches me roaming the farm alone, she's sure to know that I'm up to some mischief. But, what if I'm not alone? The Pig! Ha! That pathetic Pig will serve some purpose after all." Fixity Fox turns back and meets up with Pouting Pig.

"Mr. Fox, I thought you had left me!" Pig cries out. "Where did you go?"

"I had to run ahead to make sure the coast was clear. Now stay here behind this tree while I greet a good friend of mine," says Fixity Fox as he turns back toward the barking to face Lovable Lab.

As Lovable Lab reaches Fixity Fox, for appearance's sake, he smiles and calls out, "Hello, Lab, my good friend!"

Lovable Lab seeing Fixity Fox first, then Pouting Pig peering from behind the tree, growls, "Leave Pouting Pig alone, scoundrel, and turn away from the farm!"

Fixity Fox thinking quickly, replies, "Scoundrel? No, you don't understand, Lab. Pig and I are chums. And we're here conducting business."

"You expect me to believe that nonsense? How can a Fox be a friend of a Pig? And what business could *you* be possibly conducting, if not dirty business?"

Looking and sounding as composed as possible, Fixity Fox explains, "I am no longer the fox you used to chase away from the farm. I've turned over a new leaf. Pouting Pig has hired me to help him—I'm the little Pig's consultant."

Seeing that Lovable Lab was at least listening, Fixity Fox continues. "Pig is hopelessly depressed, for he cannot, for the life of him, understand his purpose. So, he and I are on a field trip to talk to other animals about *their* purpose on the farm."

Still seeing a skeptical look on Lovable Lab's face, Fixity Fox decides he needs to be more dramatic. "I guess a little background information is warranted. It was yesterday when I came upon the helpless Pig, and out of the goodness of my heart, I opened up my arms to save him from himself. I was out picking some berries—by the way, I'm a strict vegetarian now—and I heard him crying and squealing. This noise caused me to drop all my food and run quickly to help the poor animal. I came upon Pig and asked him what was wrong and he said that, that…" Fixity Fox stops and tries to think of something dramatic. "Pig said he was committing swineacide!"

"Swineacide?" Lovable Lab asks. "What's that?"

"The poor soul was going to take his own life!"

"How does a pig do that?"

"Well, by . . . by . . . ummm," thinks Fixity Fox as he conjures up ways Pouting Pig could take his own life. "By... by... not eating anymore! That's right! Pig said he was going to starve himself to death because he had No Purpose!" Fixity Fox pauses, then continues, "I mean, look at the little runt. You can see how thin he is. Thank heavens I was there to save him. Who knows how long he had left." For added effect, Fixity Fox bows his head as if in prayer.

Lifting his head, Fixity Fox continues, "I know it's your job to protect the animals on the farm, but I understand that you have so much to take care of, so I came to Pig's aid."

This comment surprises Lovable Lab and makes her feel irresponsible. She looks to Pouting Pig behind the tree for confirmation of Fixity Fox's story, yelling out, "Pouting Pig, do you know this Fox?"

Hearing Lovable Lab call his name, Pouting Pig pokes his head out from behind the tree and replies, "Yes, Lovable Lab, I know Mr. Fox. He's my friend!"

Using Pouting Pig's confirmation as leverage, Fixity Fox becomes more confident and says, "We've actually formed a pretty strong bond in the time we've known each other. In fact, I'll go and bring Pig to you," says Fixity Fox as he walks toward Pouting Pig.

Fixity Fox reaches Pouting Pig and says, "I called Lovable Lab from my den to let her know that we'd be coming to the farm. She's going to make sure the coast is clear for us. Remember I told you about the farmer's jealous wife? Now, come—let's go talk to Lab."

Pouting Pig moves from behind the tree and follows Fixity Fox as Fixity Fox's mind races about how he can make the most of this situation. And then something clicks in his brain. "Lovable Lab?" An ironic name, considering the nature of their relationship, but Fixity Fox realizes that Lovable Lab could be a help, not a hindrance.

Taking his notes from his pocket, Fixity Fox has an inspiration and, upon reaching Lovable Lab, says, "Pig, Lovable Lab has agreed to talk to us about **Relationships!**"

Fixity Fox continues, "Lab, you have relationships with not only the farmer and his family, but with each of the animals on the farm. Please impart your secrets of success to help our little friend build better relationships! You don't want to let this poor soul down again, do you—seeing that he had no one to turn to at his darkest hour?"

Still feeling a little guilty that Fixity Fox had saved Pouting Pig's life, Lovable Lab says, "I'll do what I can, but I wouldn't necessarily call myself an expert on relationships."

Fixity Fox responds, "Don't worry about being an expert—I've got that covered."

Fixity Fox realizes that they are in the open, and not wanting to be seen by the farmer states, "But first, let's see if any food is left over back at the trough so we can get Pig's strength back," knowing that the farmer had already fed the pigs for the morning.

"Sure," says Lovable Lab. "The farmer and his family have gone to the spring fair again today, and they'll be gone all day, so I have time to talk to the two of you."

Upon hearing this, Fixity Fox feels like kicking himself. "If I'd known that," he thinks, "I would have finished my business in the hen house and right now I'd be firing up my rotisserie and mixing some of my secret hot sauce: *Fox's Finger-lickin' Fire*. But it's too late now," laments Fixity Fox, "Still, the sooner I get this over with, the better."

When they get to the trough, all of the other pigs are asleep with their stomachs full. Pouting Pig is gleeful to find some leftover slop and begins to fill his stomach. As Pouting Pig begins to eat, Fixity Fox says, "Okay, my friend, tell Lovable Lab about your relationship problems."

Right as he fills his snout with slop, Pouting Pig says, "My parents are too busy with their jobs to listen to me and think my dreams are foolish for a pig. My brother and sister pick on me, and they always push me out of the way at the trough so I don't get enough food." After this declaration, Pouting Pig shoves his snout back into the trough.

Fixity Fox pretends to take some notes on a pad of paper and then turns to Lovable Lab. "Now you see what I'm working with here. Tell us about your relationships. What's our little Piglet doing wrong?"

"I'm not sure what he's doing wrong," replies Lovable Lab. "I haven't really thought that much about my relationships, because they just happen."

"Hmmmm..." replies Fixity Fox. Having not gotten the "answer" from Lovable Lab, he quickly looks down at his consulting research for a method to use to obtain more information from Lovable Lab. "Interesting," says Fixity Fox, as he buys time to read his research. Then he finds something—Consultant Tip #24: *The best way to get information from someone is to just keep asking questions.*

"With whom do you have relationships?" Fixity Fox asks Lovable Lab.

"My main relationships are with the farmer and his family."

"Good, tell us about these relationships."

"Well," begins Lovable Lab, "I assist the farmer. I help him round up animals that have strayed from the farm. I wake up the rest of the family when they've overslept. One night when there was a fire downstairs, I barked really loud so the family would wake up. Also, early each morning, I go with the farmer, and I help him feed the animals."

"You don't mind getting up early?" Pouting Pig asks.

"No, I like helping the farmer."

"You'd have to pay me to get up that early! I need my beauty sleep."

"I don't need money. I do it because I like doing it," replies Lovable Lab.

"Alright!" Fixity Fox says, getting excited by the exchange between Pouting Pig and Lovable Lab. "Now it sounds like we're on to something! Lab is successful in her relationships because she likes to help others. Pig does not. Therefore, Pig, I want you to write down the first Life Improvement Principle—**Principle #1: Help those that you are in a relationship with**. And do it because you like it, not because you're going to get something in return. Case in point: just like me, Pig. I am helping you out of the goodness of my heart. I understand that we cannot always accomplish things by ourselves—that we sometimes need others to help us. In a relationship, each partner needs to pitch in to help the other. Please continue, Lab."

"I'm close to the farmer's wife. I always listen to her. She talks and talks, and I listen, and then I talk back by barking."

"What else do you do while she's talking?"

"She likes it when I perk my ears up and tilt my head to let her know that I'm listening—even when I'd rather be outside catching a ball."

"Good," says Fixity Fox. "These sound like very good communication skills. Are there some communication skills you think you could improve?"

Lovable Lab thinks for a moment and responds, "At times I need to speak up more and let others know how I feel. For example, the farmer's children used to always pull my tail—and it hurt! But I didn't bark because I didn't want to scare the children. But, one day, it really hurt, so I let out a yelp as they were pulling my tail, and the farmer heard it and told the children not to pull my tail anymore. It was that simple. I had been so afraid of scaring the children that I wasn't considering my pain. I finally learned that it's not a bad thing to communicate pain."

Fixity Fox sneaks a glance at his research and responds, "Okay, it's clear that the next principle involves effectively communicating with those you are in relationships with—**Principle #2: Listen, talk, and listen some more**. This involves taking time to listen to your partner, even when you would rather be doing something else; and effective communication entails showing your partner that you are actively listening and interested in what's being said. Effective communication also involves opening up and talking about things that may be bothering you—do not hold things inside thinking that your partner knows what's bothering you. Go on Lab, what else do you do that the family likes?"

"Whenever I wag my tail, it makes the family happy. Even when I've had a long day and I'd rather be sleeping in the late afternoon sun, I wag my tail and look happy because I know the family likes it. And they also like it when I jump up and down when they come home from being away."

Fixity Fox turns to Pouting Pig, "Do you wag your tail to show your family that you like them?"

"Wag my tail? My tail is short and all curly. I'm not sure I can make it wag!" Pouting Pig says as he tries to wiggle his tail, but instead, ends up just twitching his backside.

"Well, learn! Weren't you listening? Write down this next principle—**Principle #3: Show others that you appreciate them**. And wagging your tail, not your pork butt, is a good start!" Fixity Fox exclaims.

"Now Lab, you make your relationships sound too good," continues Fixity Fox, "Tell me when you don't get along with the family."

Lovable Lab thinks for a moment. "When I was a puppy, I used to chew the farmer's wife's shoes and she would scold me. Or, sometimes I get so excited to see the family that I knock something over."

“Ahhh, I’m sure the family punishes you,” says Fixity Fox hoping to confirm that there were times when the family didn’t like Lovable Lab.

“My parents would surely punish me if I did something like that,” Pouting Pig interrupts. “So, if I knocked something over and they didn’t see me, I’d blame it on my sister or brother,” giggled Pouting Pig. “Do you have any brothers and sisters you can blame, Lab?”

“I don’t need to blame anyone, because the family doesn’t punish me. Because when I do wrong, I try to make up for my mistakes by cleaning up the mess I made and letting the family know I’m sorry.”

Disappointed that Lovable Lab doesn’t get punished, Fixity Fox says, “Pig, this is a clear example of why you’re in such bad shape. Lovable Lab acknowledges when she is wrong, yet you try to dodge responsibility and place the blame on others. Pig, you need to practice the next principle—**Principle #4: Acknowledge your mistakes and learn to say sorry.**”

“Well, my sister and brother do me wrong all the time and they never say sorry. So, I keep a list of all the bad things they’ve done to me so I can do just as many bad things back to them.”

“The good thing about the family,” says Lovable Lab, “Is that no matter how many times I knock something over, they don’t hold it against me.”

“Good point,” says Fixity Fox, “When you’re in a relationship, you should not keep reminding others about what they’ve done wrong. This will be our next principle—**Principle #5: Forgive and do not keep a running tally.**”

“A ‘running taffy’—is that candy?” Pouting Pig asks as he licks up the last of the slop.

Ignoring Pouting Pig, Fixity Fox, still looking for some of Lovable Lab’s negative relationship experiences, asks, “Lab, there must be some times when you’ve had a bad relationship—right?”

Lovable Lab thinks for a moment and says, “There was a time when I had some problems with the dog from the farm next door, Leonard the Lab. He and all of his friends kept running through the farmer’s yard on their way to the swimming pond, trampling the farmer’s wife’s flowers, and the farmer's wife thought I was the one causing the damage. So I talked to Leonard about the issue, and asked him if he could take a different route to the pond. Initially, he didn't want to take another route because it was shorter to cut through the yard. However, after much discussion, we compromised, and Leonard agreed that from then on, he would have his buddies meet him at the pond and he would walk, not run, through the farmer's yard. And something else happened—we actually ended up liking each other, and now we have a date to go out."

"Great," says Fixity Fox, once again masking his disappointment that the example had a happy ending. "Sounds like another good principle—**Principle #6: Look for opportunities to compromise."**

Fixity Fox asks Lovable Lab, "Do the principles I mentioned sound correct? Are these reasons why you are successful when it comes to relationships?"

Lovable Lab thinks of all that Fixity Fox has summarized and states, "I've never thought about my relationships in the way you describe. I guess it comes naturally. But what you said sounds accurate."

"That's not fair! It doesn't come naturally to me! How can I be expected to have good relationships when I'm not lovable like you? I mean, I can't even wag my tail!" Pouting Pig whines as he slumps on the ground.

Fixity Fox says sternly, "Buck up, Pig. That crying will get you nowhere."

"Don't be so hard on Pouting Pig," responds Lovable Lab as she goes to comfort him. "Now that you've told him about relationships, all he has to do is work on his. And I'll help him."

"You will?" Pouting Pig asks as Lovable Lab nuzzles up to him.

Fixity Fox, seeing the affection between Lovable Lab and Pouting Pig, and feeling left out, says, "Pig, that's exactly what I was going to tell you with the last principle of relationships—**Principle #7: Make the effort to ensure your relationships work**. Because having good relationships does not always come naturally. And we will *both* help you work on yours."

At this time, Lovable Lab sees Leonard the Lab in the distance and says she has to leave to tend to her own relationship. "Call me if you need me," she says as she runs off. "And stay away from that hen house, Mr. Fox, or I'll show you how our now good relationship can turn into a bad relationship very quickly!"

Fixity Fox and Pouting Pig thank Lovable Lab. Fixity Fox then reflects on how Lovable Lab respected his input and thinks, "I like being an expert. Plus, Lovable Lab won't be so suspicious of me in the future, which means easy access to my meals!" He ponders what else he can gain from this new relationship.

Pouting Pig interrupts Fixity Fox's scheming, "You really had some good information about relationships Mr. Fox. I bet you have really great relationships."

The comment catches Fixity Fox off guard. He pauses and thinks about his relationships and realizes that at this point in his life, he really doesn't have any substantial relationships—he's essentially a loner. He doesn't let others get close to him, and he's always working on some scheme and doesn't want to be distracted. He acknowledges to himself that he does get lonely at times, and he remembers feeling the twinge of jealously listening to how much the family loved Lovable Lab, whereas he has always been seen as a scoundrel and an outcast.

"Are you okay Mr. Fox?"

Fixity Fox shakes off his thoughts and replies, "Of course. And keep in mind that this trip is about *your* relationships, not mine. You're the one in desperate need of fixing."

"I liked talking to Lovable Lab! Who are we going to talk to now?" Pouting Pig asks with anticipation.

Not knowing the answer to Pouting Pig's question, Fixity Fox realizes that while Pouting Pig had a chance to eat, his own stomach was starting to growl. He decided that he needed to buy some time, and also see if there was something he could find to eat to tide him over until he was done with Pouting Pig. He sees a stable nearby and says, "Let's go to the stables and prepare for our next interview."

With that, the two trot off for the next phase of their journey.

Fixity Fox's Life Principles—Relationships

(With a little help from the Lovable Lab)

- Principle #1: Communicate: Listen, Talk, Listen Some More.
- Principle #2: Show Others That You Appreciate Them.
- Principle #3: Help Those You are in Relationships With.
- Principle #4: Acknowledge Your Mistakes and Say Sorry.
- Principle #5: Forgive and Do Not Keep a Tally.
- Principle #6: Look for Opportunities to Compromise.
- Principle #7: Make the Effort to Ensure Your Relationships Work.

(Note: Fixity Fox will provide additional information in Chapter 8 regarding specific actions related to these principles.)

Reader Reflection:

Let me start with a series of questions I would like you to think about: How important are relationships to you? What characteristics of the Lovable Lab do you see in yourself? Do relationships come naturally to you? Do you like helping those in your life? Are you an effective communicator—are you a good listener; do you express yourself freely in your relationships, or do you let others pull your tail without protest because you might offend them?

Overall, are you satisfied with your relationships? Or, are you sometimes so frustrated with your relationships that you feel like you're chasing your own tail?

Look at the list of relationship principles again. They sound fairly simple, don't they? But alas, simple isn't synonymous with easy! How often do people in relationships practice these seemingly *simple* principles? **Assignment 1:** Think about some of your good relationships, and some of your not-so-good relationships. Write down some of these relationships. For example: *Good: Me and (Insert name). Not so Good: Me and (Insert name).* Now compare which relationship principles were met/not met (by either you or your partner) in the good relationships, and which were met/not met in the not so good relationships. Do you see a difference between the two types of relationships?

It's time to be honest with yourself while conducting **Assignment 2:** I want you to rate yourself on the following: which of the principles do you practice currently, and which could you do a better job at doing in your current relationships? If your partner or friends were to judge your performance on the principles, would they agree with how you rated yourself? Why not do this simple assignment and find out?

After you've completed the assignments, let's learn about the next Life Aspect—**Career**.

Chapter 3: Life Aspect—Career

Work hard my friend, do what you do best;
Pursue a talent, work for yourself, or be employed.
If your goal is to be successful and fulfilled,
Strive to do what you enjoyed.

Fixity Fox and Pouting Pig go to the stables and look inside. There are two show horses in the stalls, and buckets of grain hang on the stall doors. Fixity Fox decides that grains aren't his cup of tea, so he stops at the door to refer to his research to help him decide what animal to talk to next.

Pouting Pig, however, rushes ahead and digs into one of the buckets. A show horse with a shimmering silver mane sees Pouting Pig and neighs, "Eww, eww… filthy! Filthy swine!"

"Oh, I'm sowwy horsey. I didn't know this was your lunch!" Pouting Pig apologizes.

"It's too late now, Pig, you can continue to eat, because I won't eat after a swine," replies the horse. The horse in the other stall starts laughing, and the two horses continue a conversation they were having.

"I can't image working in those hot fields day in, and day out, like those *work horses*. Their coats are so dull, and their hooves are always dirty from plowing and dragging and pulling and lifting. How dreadful!"

The second show horse replies, as she looks at her reflection in the trophy shelved in her stall, "Well, if I were a work horse, I … well, nothing really. Look at me, I couldn't be a work horse even if it was Halloween and I wore a costume." Both horses laugh loudly.

Fixity Fox, overhearing the conversation from the doorway, and knowing the horses being referred to, immediately knows his next move. On all fours, so the horses can't see him over their stall doors, he glances around the stable looking for Pouting Pig and finds him with his ham hocks twitching in the air, his head stuck in a bucket of grain. Fixity Fox grabs Pouting Pig and motions that it's time for them to leave.

"But why?" Pouting Pig whines. "I'm not done."

Fixity Fox responds in a hushed tone, "We have an appointment with some work horses, and we don't want to be late."

Once outside the stable, Fixity Fox turns to Pouting Pig, "We're going to talk to the horses about the value of having a job!"

Fixity Fox and Pouting Pig walk to the field where two horses wearing blinders are pulling a plow. They sit on a fence and watch the two horses plow straight furrows in the land. As they watch, Fixity Fox begins explaining how what the horses are doing represents the next Life Aspect—**Career**.

“Pig, we’re now going to talk about the value of having a career. As you probably know, these horses are the hardest working animals on the farm. To them, their purpose in life is working for a living. While the Lovable Lab was valued by the farmer for companionship and relationships, the farmer values the horses because of the outstanding job they do working around the farm and in the fields.”

Fixity Fox goes on to explain, “To some animals, the work they do is secondary in their lives; however, to other animals, the work they do defines who they are. Take me, for example—I am known as a world-renowned consultant, who sometimes performs pro-bono work for unfortunate creatures like yourself. When animals hear the name ‘Fixity Fox,’ they instantly think of a master consultant. Pig, what do you do for a living? What do you want to be known for?”

“Well,” begins Pouting Pig as he thinks, “I don’t do *anything* for a living—unless eating counts.”

“No, eating doesn’t count—unless you’re Horse Forman, maker of the Horse Forman Grill. But since you don’t work, at some point you’ll need to get off your rump roast and contribute to society by doing something productive. Because one day, God forbid, you may have a family, and you’ll need to support them by bringing home the bacon.”

“The bacon?” Pouting Pig asks, looking confused.

“Umm, never mind,” replies Fixity Fox.

About this time, the horses take a break and come over to the fence to see what a fox could possibly be doing with a pig. Fixity Fox introduces himself as the horses pull up their blinders and warily look the two over. The horses introduce themselves as the “Hardworking Horses,” a husband-and-wife team.

Fixity Fox begins by explaining, “I can see the confusion in your eyes, Hardworking Horses, but fret not. I am a consultant helping Pig improve his life because he has no purpose. One thing that would give the little fella some purpose, something to get him out of bed in the morning, would be a good job. I wanted to talk to the two of you about the importance of making a living and having a career. So, answer us this: What makes you two so successful at what you do?"

The husband, still not completely trusting Fixity Fox, responds in a pronounced drawl, "Well, I reckon you can say we're successful in our job, as you say there Mr. Fox. But there ain't no secret to it. My wife and I, well, we just come out here every day, bust our humps and do our jobs. That's pretty much all there is to it." The husband looks at his wife, and she nods her head in confirmation.

"I see," says Fixity Fox, realizing once again that he was going to have to get better at getting his "experts" to open up. "Tell me about a typical work day for the two of you," prods Fixity Fox.

Eager to talk, the wife begins, "Our day begins at 5:00 a.m., when we help the farmer drag the food bins around to all of the other animals so they can eat."

"Do you do this every day?" Fixity Fox asks.

"Sure as sin," replies the husband.

"Rain or shine," continues the wife. "And after the animals are fed, the farmer puts the harness on us and we begin plowing the field to prepare it for his spring planting."

Remembering some of the research he saw on trends in the workplace, Fixity Fox asks, "Excuse me for asking, but you both seem a tad bit old to still be plowing. Are you worried that the farmer may replace you with technology? Or outsource your work?"

"Watch yer mouth there, Fox!" The husband snorts as he shakes his neck and mane. "You better know how to swim 'cause you're skating on some very thin ice! If I didn't know better, I'd take you as one of those types of consultants that come in and recommend that a mess of folks get fired!"

"No, no, not at all. My only goal is to help Pig here. You can trust me on that. I was just curious."

After some hesitation the husband continues, "Well, to answer your question, we had one 'em new fangled tractors here once. Remember that dagblasted thing?" asks the husband turning to his wife.

"Of course, and the time it rained for an entire week!" The husband and wife both begin laugh.

"The farmer had placed the wife and me into 'early retirement' or so he called it, but when that rain came down, and that tractor got stuck in the mud, with its wheels spinning like there was no tomorrow, guess who he called back into service?" The husband asks triumphantly. "That's right. It was us good 'ole reliable Hardworking Horses to the rescue! In fact, the farmer relies on us so much now, he trusts us to plow the field by ourselves while he's not here."

"That's right," the wife chimes in. "But even after the tractor incident, the farmer still had to learn the hard way. He tried to replace us with some other horses and it didn't work. He brought in a team of young horses right out of school to help out because he said it was going to be a busy year. And at first they looked impressive—"

"Right," interjects the husband, "With their new harnesses and neatly groomed manes and all. And their fancy M-B-As."

"MBAs?" Fox asks.

"Masters of Better Agriculture," sniffs the husband. "I tell you, them degrees ain't worth the paper they're printed on."

"He's right, because even with all that education, they didn't do good work," finishes the wife.

The husband adds, "She's darn right, the furrows weren't deep enough, and they spaced them too far apart so they had less to plow. They thought my eyes were bad and I wouldn't notice that they were cutting corners. And I tell you sumthin' else, them youngsters were more interested in prancing 'round in front of them highfalutin' show horses than doing good work. In the end, we had to go back and re-do the work they had done."

“I see,” responds Fixity Fox, feeling a little guilty, knowing that he had cut his share of corners in his day.

He turns to Pouting Pig, “Did you catch what the horses said? Whatever you end up doing for your career, do it right. This will be the first principle of the Career Life Aspect—**Principle #8: Work hard and do good work**.”

Fixity Fox asks the horses, “What else does the farmer have you do?”

“Actually,” begins the wife, “There are times when the farmer doesn’t have work for us, so we look around the farm and see what we can do ourselves—like the time we had that big storm last August.”

“September. It was in September,” corrects the husband.

“Anyway,” continues the wife, “A huge tree fell down in the road during the storm, and after the storm was over, I suggested to my husband that we should go and move it so the farmer could take his crop to market.”

“Hold on now,” says the husband, “I was the one that said we should move that daggone tree!”

“Sure, sure,” retorts the wife, “You always try to take credit. But anyway, regardless of whose idea it was, we moved the tree and the farmer was very thankful.”

“Pig, write this down,” says Fixity Fox. “The next key to a successful career is—**Principle #9: Take initiative**.”

Pouting Pig begins to write, then stops and says, “Mr. Fox, how do you spell ‘initiative’? And what does it mean?”

“Initiative means doing something before you’re asked to do it. Being proactive.”

“Proact—?” Pouting Pig begins.

Fixity Fox interrupts and says to the horses, “You’ll have to excuse my little friend here, he’s not the sharpest tool in the shed. But please go on, what else makes the two of you successful?”

"Well," says the wife, "Even though my husband has memory problems, surprisingly enough, we do work well together."

"Please explain."

"We complement each other. For example, my husband is stronger than I am; however, he likes to rush through the work, but if we go too fast, the work is sloppy. So I slow us down and make sure that the furrows we plow are straight. By combining our strengths, the result is a perfectly plowed field."

"Yes, I'll admit, the wife is a bit neater than I am. But another good thing about working with the missus is that we pick up each other's slack. For example, last planting season, my wife here got hoof and mouth disease—"

"How many times do I have to tell you? Horses don't get hoof and mouth disease!" exclaims the wife.

"Well, whatever it was, the wife was sick and was down for a few days, and I worked extra hours to make up for her not being here so the farmer could get the crops planted in time."

The wife counters, "Let's not forget the time you had a tiny nail in your hoof and called in sick claiming you couldn't walk, and I had to pull the cart by myself for three days!"

Fixity Fox interrupts the two horses, "In spite of your squabbling, it sounds like the two of you are a regular Dynamic Duo—one that practices good teamwork."

Turning to Pouting Pig, Fixity Fox continues, "Pig, you may need to work with a group of people, and to be successful, the group will need to work together. This is called teamwork. Being part of a good team involves working with team members that help and complement each other. Write this down as the next principle—**Principle #10: Be a good team player**."

The husband continues, "Another important thing about our work is that what we do helps others."

"That's right," agrees the wife. "After we plow the field, the farmer can plant his crop. And the results are fields of food that the farmer uses to feed his family and many others when he takes the produce to market. We really take a lot of pride in this."

The husband adds, "I sure get a sense of fulfillment when the wife and I pull a fully loaded cart into town seeing all of our hard work come to fruition. I ask you, can those stuck-up Show Horses say the same thing? What's the benefit of what they do?"

"Okay," says Fixity Fox. "**Principle #11: Be proud of what you do** is the next principle of having a good career. This can lead to a sense of self-fulfillment. What do you think about that, Pig?"

Pouting Pig responds excitedly, "I wanna help the horses plow the field because I want to feed a lot of people too!"

"Oh, don't worry—you'll feed others." Fixity Fox mummers under his breath.

"I guess what I like most about our job," says the husband, "Is that at the end of the day, Mr. Fox, the long and short of it is, we just plain like what we do. We wouldn't want to do anything else."

"Correct," adds the wife. "There are some horses that spend their lives racing around a track, or carrying people on their backs—"

"Or looking all pretty so they can jump them little fences and try to collect trophies," sniffs the husband.

"We would just *hate* doing that. But we like working in the field. We truly enjoy what we do," finishes the wife.

"Excellent! We will make that the last and most important item on the list. To truly be successful in your career—**Principle #12: Enjoy your work**," says Fixity Fox.

"Oh no! Look at that, we've gone over our break by three minutes," the wife says. "We better get back to work."

"Now don't get your harness all twisted in a bunch, honey, I can make it up by plowing a little faster."

"How many times have I told you we're not going to race through our work? You're as stubborn as a mule," says the wife turning toward Fixity Fox and Pouting Pig. "It's a full-time job just trying to manage this old guy."

"Nag, nag, nag," replies the husband.

"But you love it," says the wife as they put their blinders back on.

"Thank you very much for your time," says Fixity Fox.

"Yeah!" adds Pouting Pig. "Let me know when I can come and help plow the field."

The wife responds, "Sure, Pouting Pig. And thank you, Mr. Fox. When you're done with your research, we'd really like to take a look at what you find that can help us work even better and more efficiently."

"Of course," replies Fixity Fox, feeling a sense of pride that the horses wanted his research.

As the horses walk off, Fixity Fox thinks to himself, "I better start writing this information down for real," and he takes quick notes on the career-related principles he had just discussed with the horses.

As he writes, Fixity Fox turns to Pouting Pig, "Did you write all that down Pig? And are you motivated enough to go and get a job and make something out of yourself?"

"I guess. I just need to find something I'm good at." Pouting Pig pauses and then asks, "Mr. Fox, are you proud of what you do for a living?"

Once again Fixity Fix is thrown off by Pouting Pig's question. He looks back over his "career," and realizes that it consisted primarily of devising clever schemes to get things he wanted. There was the time he tried to obtain a fried chicken franchise so he would have unlimited access to all the *original recipe* and *crispy* his heart desired. And then one Thanksgiving, he dressed up in a Pilgrim costume and went to the supermarket so he could hand out turkeys (and keep a few for himself of course). Not necessarily a career to be proud of.

"But why does Pig keep asking these irritating questions?" Fixity Fox wonders. "This trip is about helping Pig, not helping me."

Fixity Fox also begins realizing that while at first he wanted to get this charity exercise over as quickly as possible, he is now actually enjoying this adventure. He is surprised at how well he is able to take what the animals say and quickly summarize key points into a concise picture of what was important to them and what made them successful. And, he likes the feeling that the animals respected him and his input. This is much better than being seen as a chicken-coop-robbing-scoundrel.

Fixity Fox straightens his jacket, presses down on the edges of his name tag and replies to Pouting Pig, "I'm very proud of my career, my little friend. Now—we have two Life Aspects down, and two more to go. Then, as promised, you'll be a pouter no more."

"But, it's hot," complains Pouting Pig. "And I'm tired. Can we just rest for a while?"

Fixity Fox agrees to Pouting Pig's request so that he would have time to think about which animal they should visit next. He sees an abandoned barn in the distance, and the two set off towards it.

Fixity Fox's Life Principles—Career

(With input from the Hardworking Horses)

- Principle #8: Work Hard and Do Good Work.
- Principle #9: Take Initiative.
- Principle #10: Be a Good Team Player.
- Principle #11: Be Proud of What You Do.
- Principle #12: Enjoy Your Work.

(Note: Fixity Fox will provide additional information in Chapter 8 regarding specific actions related to these principles.)

Reader Reflection:

How important is your career to you? Would you consider yourself a hard-working horse? Do you find that your work takes precedence over other things in your life? If so, are you okay with this? Are others in your life okay with this?

Notice that because of the horses' excellent work ethic, the farmer realized that they were indispensable. Are you indispensable where you work? Or, can you be easily replaced or outsourced? If so, are there things you can do to change this?

Notice how the husband and wife were a bit competitive and wanted to take credit themselves for everything. Does this happen in your workplace with your co-workers? Are you competitive at work? Is this a good or bad trait to have?

Glance at the first three Career principles. How would you score in terms of them on a performance review given by your boss and co-workers? **Assignment 1:** Write down examples where you've exhibited each of these three principles in the last year. Was this easy or difficult to do? Once again, be honest with yourself—as the well-known phrase goes, "Are you hard working, or hardly working?" A question I like to ask people is, "If you owned the company, would you hire someone like yourself as an employee?"

Granted, some of our less-than-satisfactory job performance is a result of our dissatisfaction with our job. Look at the last two principles and perform **Assignment 2:** Ask yourself—"*Am I proud of what I do? Do I enjoy what I do?*" If you answered "No" to both of those questions, finish the assignment by asking yourself, "*Am I willing to do something about it?*" Think about your answers, and when you're ready—let's learn about the next Life Aspect—**Self**.

Chapter 4: Life Aspect—Self

How do I look, and how do I feel about myself?
If I were a tree, what kind of tree would I be?
What makes me tick, and how am I perceived?
All in all, get used to saying "I like being me!"

Inside the "abandoned" barn, Confident Cat puts on his camouflage hunting clothes. "I'm going to catch the biggest mouse ever today!" He exclaims.

"You disgust me with all your macho bravado!" retorts Conscience Cat. "You should really give up your carnivorous ways and live a more natural lifestyle that includes not eating meat."

"What, and be a nature-loving tree-hugger like yourself? Scratch that! Never in a million years!"

"Please! Will the two of you keep it down? I'm trying to concentrate on my painting while the others aren't here!" Creative Cat hisses.

"I'm on my way out anyway. I'll be returning with my trophy catch shortly!" Confident Cat boasts as he tightens his hunting headband around his head.

Outside, Fixity Fox and Pouting Pig sit down against the barn to rest. "Read over what you've learned so far Pig. There's going to be a test on this material."

"I hate tests," complains Pouting Pig as he begins to pour over his sloppily written notes. Fixity Fox turns his attention to his list to determine which Life Aspects were left to discuss: *Self* and *Spirituality*.

Fixity Fox thinks, "What animal can I talk to next? So far I've gotten lucky and picking the animals has taken care of itself. What if, instead of talking to more animals, I just make up some smart-sounding wisdom and send Pig on his way? I've lived up to my side of the deal, and surely Pig will be happy to have received so much attention." But Fixity Fox remembers what the horses said earlier about cutting corners, and decides he really does want to see this endeavor through.

"The more I learn from the animals, the smarter I'll get," thinks Fixity Fox. "Then, who knows? I could take this show on the road. Surely every farm has some down-and-out animal who needs help and would be willing to pay a small sum to get fixed. Or better yet, to make big bucks, I could do what other famous animals have done. What if I had my own daytime talk show like *Osprey Winfrey*? Or wrote self-help books like *Dr. Eel*? Then I'd have enough money to buy my own television station. I could call it the *Fox Channel*!"

Fixity Fox daydreams for a moment about future riches and thinks, "First let me finish with Pig. Now where was I? That's right, I need to identify some more animals to talk to." Fixity Fox looks out to the pasture and sees a herd of cows eating grass. "What's left on my list? Self and Spirituality? Hmmm, cows are spiritual animals in some countries. Maybe we should go and chat with them." Fox imagines discussing spirituality with a cow chewing a mouthful of grass while salvia runs from its mouth, then rules it out.

As Fixity Fox thinks about which topic to tackle next, he twitches his tail in deep thought. Suddenly, he feels a sharp pain on his tail, followed quickly by a loud "Gotcha!" Fox leaps up startled, and looks back to see a cat wearing a camouflage jacket and a headband around his head still holding on to his tail.

"What the—" begins Fixity Fox.

"I'm the best hunter on the farm, and I've just captured you!" Confident Cat boasts.

With a strong yank, Fixity Fox frees himself from Confident Cat's grasp. "I strongly beg to differ," retorts Fixity Fox. "In fact, I could out-hunt you wearing combat boots three sizes too big and big fat bells hanging around my neck! You sure are overly confident, aren't you?"

"That's why they call me Confident Cat! I can do whatever I put my mind to. Like they say, 'A brain is a terrible thing to waste'!"

"I wish I were confident," says Pouting Pig, impressed by Confident Cat.

"You just have to believe in yourself. If you can believe it, you can achieve it!" responds Confident Cat.

Fixity Fox was about to tell Confident Cat to stop with the slogans and self-help book affirmations, but then realizes that the cat had come along just at the right time.

"I see that you have a really high opinion of yourself, my little feline friend. Would you mind telling me what's most important in your life?"

"Sure! I'm very focused and centered in what I do, and I strive every day to improve myself. I want to be all that I can be."

"Interesting," replies Fixity Fox as he checks the **Self** Life Aspect off his list. "So you're into constantly improving yourself. In what ways? Mentally? Creatively? Financially?"

"No way! Who has time for all of that? I focus on being the most confident cat on the farm and maintaining my physical superiority. But you might want to talk to some of my brothers and sisters if you want to know about those other things. Follow me, and I can tell you more about me as well."

Fixity Fox and Pouting Pig follow Confident Cat into the barn, where over the door was the following sign: "*Welcome to the Home of the Centered Cats.*"

Once inside, Fixity Fox and Pouting Pig see two more members of the family.

"Hey everybody," begins Confident Cat, "Mr. Fox and Pouting Pig want to talk to me about how great I am!"

Confident Cat introduces his siblings. "This is my sister Creative Cat; she thinks she's a great painter," as he points to his first sister who is painting a picture with her tail. "And this is my other sister, Conscience Cat. She's a militant!" He says, as he points to his second sister, who is making a sign with the words "Save the Mice" on it.

"I am not a militant!" Conscience Cat shouts. "I'm just very passionate about my causes, and most animals don't understand my causes because their level of conscience isn't high enough. Or in your case, your IQ isn't high enough. All that weightlifting you do has hardened that muscle between your ears!"

"I'm rubber and you're glue, what you say bounces off me and sticks to you!" Confident Cat counters in a sing-song voice.

Fixity Fox, observing the exchange between the cats, wonders what he's gotten himself into.

"Don't mind the two of them," replies Creative Cat. "Please, sit down, Mr. Fox and Pouting Pig. Let me paint the two of you. I'll start with you, Mr. Fox."

As they sit next to each other, Confident Cat tells his sisters, "Isn't it great that Mr. Fox wants to talk to me?" Then turning to Fixity Fox, he says, "Mr. Fox, where do you want me to start?"

Fixity Fox watches Confident Cat as he takes off his camouflage jacket and headband and puts a weightlifting belt around his waist. Fixity Fox thinks how he would like to take Confident Cat by the tail and twirl him around a few times. But instead, feigning interest, he says, "Tell me more about how you feel about yourself and what motivates you."

"That's easy, I want to look good and feel good. I take care of myself because my body is a temple. If you don't love yourself, no one else will."

"Okay, okay we get the picture," says Fixity Fox rolling his eyes. "And what else is important to you?"

"I want to be the King of the Jungle, just like a lion is!"

"Do we live near a jungle?" Pouting Pig asks. "I heard there are snakes in the jungle—and I'm afraid of snakes!"

"Continue please, Cat." Fixity Fox says as he sneaks a pawful of berries from Creative Cat's paint tray to quell his rumbling stomach.

"Stay still, Mr. Fox," admonishes Creative Cat.

"Well, I want to be like a lion," continues Confident Cat. "In fact listen to this, I'm learning how to roar instead of purr." Confident Cat takes a deep breath, holds it for a second then exhales, letting out a funny sounding "roar."

Both sisters giggle at Confident Cat's attempt to roar, and Fixity Fox laughs as well. "Well Pig, I think what we've learned is: (1) Cats can't roar, and (2) No matter what others may think about you, practice the first principle of the Self Life Aspect—**Principle #13: Have a positive self-image**. Self-image includes how you feel about yourself. Are you confident or not? Do you think you're capable in many things? It also includes how comfortable you are with how you look. And if you don't like the way you look, what are you doing about it?"

"I also like to weight-lift," interrupts Confident Cat. "I work out six days a week. And while most cats drink plain milk, I drink protein shakes to build my muscles."

Fixity Fox says, “Okay, this then will be our next principle of the Self Life Aspect—**Principle #14: Take care of your body**. Pig what kind of exercise do you do?”

“Gee, I don’t know. I chase my tail a lot,” says Pouting Pig. “That gets me all sweaty and out of breath. Does that count as exercise?”

Fixity Fox refrains from making a crude comment about chasing tail as Creative Cat joins the conversation, “Exercising your body is definitely important, but so is exercising your creativity.”

Eager to move the conversation off of Confident Cat, Fixity Fox asks Creative Cat, “How does one exercise his or her creativity?”

“By pursuing the talents one has,” responds Creative Cat as she continues to paint Fixity Fox. “For example, I’m focusing on my hobby—painting.”

“What’s the benefit of having hobbies?” Fixity Fox asks because he never had any hobbies of his own. “Isn’t ‘hobby’ just another word for fun and games?”

“No, not at all,” replies Creative Cat. “Right now painting is a hobby, but I expect to make it my vocation once I get established. Also, hobbies can bring out the creative energy that we all have. And because of these hobbies, the world is a richer place. Think about the famous cat Pawblo PiCatto. Painting was his hobby, and now his works are masterpieces. But there are other types of hobbies as well: building things, collecting stamps, sewing, musical pursuits, restoring an old ’71 Catillac, etc. Performing these activities fulfills your creative self.”

Fixity Fox says, “This then will be the next principle of the Self Life Aspect—**Principle #15: Exercise your creativity**. And it’s important to note that this creativity can be expressed in the hobbies you pursue, as well as the work you do.”

“Hunting’s my hobby,” interjects Confident Cat as he curls barbells.

“I roll around in the mud a lot,” adds Pouting Pig. “Is that a hobby?”

“It depends,” says Creative Cat. “Do you enjoy it?”

“I sure do!”

“Then it’s a fulfilling hobby. Now, Pig, let me paint your picture.”

At this time, a cat wearing a green eye shade, and one wearing green eyeliner, enter the barn. "As long as you make money on your hobby," says the cat with the green eyeshade. "When are you going to sell a painting of yours, Creative Cat, so you can contribute to the rent?"

Confident Cat says, "Mr. Fox and Pouting Pig, meet my brother Cash-is-King Cat and my sister Coquette Cat. Mr. Fox and Pig want to hear about what's important to us," says Confident Cat to his brother and sister.

"Well, I'm the financial genius of the family, and you can call me Cash Cat for short. I focus on ensuring that the family's finances are in order. If it weren't for me, we'd all be stray cats out on the street."

"Why do you say that?" Fixity Fox asks.

"Well, Conscience Cat over there donates all her money to charities and buys expensive organic food. Creative Cat buys fancy art supplies. Confident Cat wastes money on all the miracle muscle powders and exercise equipment he buys from those infomercials, and Coquette Cat spends an ungodly amount of money on clothes and perfume. But, I have each one of them tell me what their financial goals are, and then I make sure each of them sets aside a certain amount every month as part of their financial plan. I'm rather proficient at giving financial advice to numerous animals on the farm. How do you think Cash Cow got rich?"

"This is good!" says Fixity Fox, who is pleased to meet a cat with principles near and dear to his own heart. "Our next principle will be—

Principle #16: Practice financial discipline. Pig, what do you wish you had money for?"

"I wish I could afford to go to Hollywood like that other Pig did and be in a movie!"

"When Pigs fly," thinks Fixity Fox. Then out loud, "Okay then, each month, put away a certain amount of money to get there."

"For a small fee, I can be your financial advisor," adds Cash Cat.

"Wow, I've got a *Life Improvement Consultant* and a *Financial Advisor* now. I feel important!"

Coquette Cat pats Pouting Pig on the head and says, "What a cute little Pig," and moves toward Fixity Fox. "Mr. Fox, you look like a gentleman that knows about money," purrs Coquette Cat as she brushes against Fixity Fox. "Because you look like a million bucks in that fur coat of yours," she says as she runs her paw through Fixity Fox's fur.

"Well, I, ummm, well…" stammers Fixity Fox, a bit uncomfortable.

"Cat got your tongue, Mr. Fox?" Coquette Cat asks, still standing close to Fixity Fox.

"Of course not! I must have gotten a fur ball in my throat. It must be all these damn cats!" Fixity Fox replies adamantly. "So where were we? Why don't you tell us what's important to you, Coquette Cat."

"For starters, I think all my brothers and sisters take life a bit too seriously! They need to live a little and love a little. Enjoy those around us. And I agree with my brother Cocky Cat—"

"Confident Cat! My name is Confident Cat!"

"Like I was saying, I agree with my brother when he says it's important to look good, but there's nothing wrong with, as my brother would say, using what you've got, to get what you want!" Coquette Cat says, winking at Fixity Fox.

Uncomfortable with Coquette's comments, Fixity Fox responds, "Let's not corrupt the impressionable Pig. Can you explain—in a G-rated manner please—how you would sum up what's important to you?"

"Sure, as you can probably tell, I'm a very sensual pussycat. Some cats act so neutered because they're ashamed of their bodies or urges they may have. Or, they were told by their parents and society certain things about what's right and what's wrong with their sexuality. But I'm not ashamed of my body or my feelings and urges because I'm comfortable with my sensuality. And, I like to flirt a bit. So, cute little Pig, I want you to add this to the list you're writing—**Principle #17: Be secure in your sensuality**."

"Sure," says Pouting Pig pleased with the compliment he received. "But what does 'sensuality' mean?"

"I'll tell you later Pig," Fixity Fox quickly says, as Creative Cat finishes Pouting Pig's painting and begins to play a song on a musical instrument.

"More cowbell!" Confident Cat shouts, as the others laugh at the joke.

At this time, another cat, wearing glasses and a bow tie, comes in the barn carrying a stack of books with a glass of milk balanced on the top. Fixity Fox thinks, "If another cat walks in that door, I'll go crazy!"

Confident Cat says, "Mr. Fox, meet my other brother, Cerebral Cat." Cerebral Cat extends his hand to greet Fox and causes the glass of milk to tip over on Coquette Cat.

"Oh, oh, oh, my beautiful, beautiful fur!" Coquette Cat exclaims. "You're so clumsy, you furball! I just paid good money to get groomed, and now it's RUINED!!!"

"You spent money on grooming? I don't remember that being in your budget," says Cash Cat as he marks this in his expense journal.

"Well, I am very sorry, Coquette," says Cerebral Cat. "However, it's quite clear that my intention was not to spill the milk on you. Now, as for your fur," Cerebral Cat opens one of the books and begins to read, "According to recent research, studies have shown that milk is full of natural lipids, proteins, and vitamins that can nourish your fur."

"It can?" Coquette Cat asks.

"Why, yes. Milk can help preserve your natural PH balance."

"Really?"

"Would I ever give you a brain tease, Coquette?"

"That wouldn't be hard!" Confident Cat interjects loudly so he could be heard over Creative Cat's music.

"You better be glad you have nine lives, muscle head, because I'm about to take one of them right now!" screams Coquette Cat, upset that her brother embarrassed her in front of Fixity Fox.

"Will everyone please keep it down in here!" Conscience Cat shouts, making even more noise. "I'm trying to write my speech for tomorrow. And if it's not Confident Cat always trying to get his two cents in, I've got to put up with Cash Cat counting his money out loud!"

Cerebral Cat adjusts his glasses and bow tie and says to Fixity Fox in a measured voice, "Excuse my extremely loud siblings, I am the most civilized member of this feline family. To what do we owe the pleasure of your visit to our humble abode?"

"I'm here asking your family what's important to them in their lives. So I will pose the same question to you. What do you find important?"

"That's a very thought-provoking question, sir. I'm sure you've had time to converse with my siblings here, and they've had time to impress upon you why what they believe is most important. But let me pose this point: While one's physical prowess diminishes, and one's looks fade, if properly engaged, the brain continues to function well into our latter years. In fact, it is the brain that regulates the other aspects of ourselves. It is because of our brain that we have the willpower to embark upon a rigorous exercise routine. It is the brain that guides us as we paint a masterpiece or write the next best selling novel."

"Good, please continue," says Fixity Fox making sure to write down all of what Cerebral Cat was saying.

"Much like a garden needs nourishment to grow and thrive, so too does a brain. A brain must be constantly fed nutrients in the form of insight, data, queries, thought-provoking ideas, and the like. The brain is a muscle that must be used and flexed just like any muscle if it is to grow. To coin a phase: A brain is a terrible thing to waste."

"Hey, scratch that! That's my line!" Confident Cat yells.

"Your points are very well-thought out Cerebral Cat," says Fixity Fox. "We'll add this as our next principle—**Principle #18: Continually engage your mind**."

Conscience Cat, who has finished working on her speech, begins preparing dinner for the family and says, "I take issue with some of what my brother said, Mr. Fox. He and I have had this discussion before, and I believe that it is one's conscience that regulates all of the other aspects of ourselves. In fact, the brain receives its cues from the conscience."

"What's a conscience, Ms. Cat?" Pouting Pig asks, as Fixity Fox leans in intently to hear the answer as well.

"A conscience tells you what's right and what's wrong. It can be a moral guidepost. Also, your conscience can give you something to stand for."

"Stand for?" Pouting Pig asks.

Conscience Cat replies, "Standing for something means believing in something. Having a cause. Being willing to *fight* for something."

"But I'm a lover not a fighter," replies Pouting Pig.

"That's a good one, Pig," says an impressed Confident Cat, as Pouting Pig beams from the encouragement.

"What's *your* cause?" Fixity Fox asks Conscience Cat.

"What isn't her cause?" Confident Cat responds. "Last week, she was supporting the BMF (Blind Mice Foundation), and the week before that it was PETA (Pets Everywhere Take Action). And next week, it will be something just as far-fetched."

"You hush!" Conscience Cat responds, her voice raising with intensity. "I'm willing to protect the less fortunate! I want to give a voice to those that can't speak for themselves—the downtrodden, the persecuted. I'm also in touch with those at the grass roots in order to affect social and political change. For example, I'm currently working on a campaign to protect the helpless mice on the farm from predators like my brother here," says Conscience Cat showing everyone the signs she made. "We're having a rally and a protest tomorrow."

"What makes you decide to take up an issue?" Fixity Fox asks.

"I let my conscience be my guide. My conscience helps me determine what I believe is right or wrong, and what's good and bad. What I feel is important to do. This includes helping others, volunteering, debating, engaging in the political process, and so forth."

"Okay, Pig, write this down as the next principle of Self—**Principle #19: Define your conscience and act accordingly**. This includes performing acts guided by your conscience."

"Do we all have a conscience? And how do we know what it is?" Pouting Pig asks.

"Each animal needs to define his or her own conscience," replies Conscience Cat.

"I don't know if I can do this. Mr. Fox, how do I do this?"

"Let's have Conscience Cat tell us," replies Fixity Fox, not knowing the answer since he had never encountered his conscience before.

"I can't tell you how to define your conscience," begins Conscience Cat. "Your conscience defines itself based on your perceptions and beliefs. For example, if you were at the market and the sales animal gave you back too much change, and she didn't realize it, would you tell her, or would you keep the extra money? Or, here's another example: Let's say you saw someone who needed help. Would you help them for the satisfaction of helping them, or would you help them hoping that they'll give you something in return?"

Fixity Fox begins to feel uncomfortable by the examples given. "Are you saying that someone is good or bad based on how they answer those questions?"

"Not necessarily," replies Conscience Cat. "It's up to each animal to make that judgment. Also, one's conscience is related somewhat to one's spirituality, because spirituality can influence one's conscience. While there's not always a direct connection, sometimes, the more spiritual a person, the more evolved their conscience. That's what the Omniscient Owl told me."

Fixity Fox thinks, "*Spirituality* and the Omniscient Owl? Great, the final piece of the puzzle has fallen into place." Then he says out loud, "That's actually who we're going to talk to about our last Life Aspect—**Spirituality**."

"Good, I'm currently learning some things from the Owl. Tell Owl I said hello."

"Will do," says Fixity Fox. "Is he where he usually is? Out by the—?" He trails off hoping that Conscience Cat will give an indication where they can find the Owl.

"Yes, *she's* at the north edge of the farm," replies Conscience Cat.

"Oh," replies Fixity Fox, a bit surprised. "Then we'll go and see her now."

"I was hoping you could stay for dinner. I'm preparing a totally organic vegan delight," says Conscience Cat with disappointment.

"So sorry, we can't stay," responds Fixity Fox, not interested in a meatless dinner. "We must be going because we have one last visit before it gets too dark." Fixity Fox and Pouting Pig then say their goodbyes and prepare to leave.

Creative Cat gives Fixity Fox and Pouting Pig their paintings.

"See you when I see you!" shouts Confident Cat.

"If you ever feel like playing chess, I'd be glad to engage in a game with you," Cerebral Cat says to Fixity Fox.

"Call me about that financial plan, Pig," says Cash Cat as he hands Pouting Pig his business card.

And as they near the door, Coquette Cat says with a deep purr, "Come and see me some time big fella," as Fixity Fox quickly passes by her.

Once outside the barn, as Fixity Fox is finishing up his notes, they hear a loud roar come from inside.

"Isn't that something?" remarks a surprised Fixity Fox, "It seems like Confident Cat kept at it. And like him or not, as he said when we first met, he believed in himself and achieved his goal. So, Pig, that is the last and most important principle of Self—no matter what—**Principle #20: Believe in yourself**."

"Okay, I'll try," says Pouting Pig as he looks down at his painting. He realizes that he is smiling in his picture and looks very happy. Fixity Fox looks at his picture and realizes that he has an unsure, pensive look on his face. In fact, he is still processing what he had learned from the cacophony of cats in the barn. Specifically, the discussion about conscience was bothering him, as are some of Pouting Pig's earlier questions. Maybe he's not as well off as he had once thought. He also feels that the next conversation would either answer the questions he had or leave him with yet more.

Fixity Fox puts his arm around Pouting Pig's pork shoulder and says, "Pig, onward and upward for our last meeting of the day. Let's go fix our, err…, I mean, fix *your* spirituality!"

Fixity Fox's Life Principles—Self

(With a herd of help from the Centered Cats)

- Principle #13 Have a Positive Self Image.
- Principle #14 Take Care of Your Body.
- Principle #15 Exercise Your Creativity.
- Principle #16 Practice Financial Discipline.
- Principle #17 Be Secure With Your Sensuality.
- Principle #18 Continually Engage Your Mind.
- Principle #19: Define Your Conscience and Act Accordingly.
- Principle #20: Believe in Yourself.

(Note: Fixity Fox will provide additional information in Chapter 8 regarding specific actions related to these principles.)

Reader Reflection:

The traits in this chapter were selected for the Self Life Aspect because they are the aspects that individuals can control within themselves. So, are you a Centered Cat, focused on one or two of the Self Life Aspects? If so which ones:

- *Do you let your mind be your guide, or your conscience be your guide? Is there a meaningful difference?*
- *Are you overly confident? If so, when might your confidence look more like cockiness?*
- *Do you live your live through affirmations and slogans? Do they help?*
- *Do you express yourself through your creativity? How?*
- *Are you comfortable with your sensuality and expressing it?*
- *How important is money to you? Do financial decisions dictate your other Self Life Aspects?*

Did you notice how many of the Self Aspects compete for attention in our lives like the cats did? Much like the "noise" in the barn with each cat vying for attention, so it is with ourselves and our internal demands and self-conflicts. Do you have time to focus on all of these competing aspects? Or, should you focus on one or two Self Life Aspects and neglect the other aspects like most of the cats did? **Assignment 1:** Identify which of your "cats" is the loudest and which "cat" is neglected. Are you okay with what you identified?

As you saw, the Self Life Aspects and other Life Aspects can overlap and affect each other. **Assignment 2**: Identify which of your Self Life Aspects affect your other Life Aspects (e.g., Career, Relationships, Spirituality). Determine if improving one of your Self Life Aspects can help improve any of your other Life Aspects.

Give that some thought, and when you're ready—on to the last Life Aspect—**Spirituality**!

Chapter 5: Life Aspect—Spirituality

A Pig asks, "What is my soul, and what does it do?"
"I'll teach you," says the Fox, lacking true knowledge of his own.
But with insight and an example set by a wise old Owl,
By the end, they'll find that they've both grown.

Omniscient Owl settles down on a branch as she waits for the two pilgrims. She has been unable to sleep today and has watched Fixity Fox and Pouting Pig speak to the animals on the farm. It's fitting that they end their journey with Omniscient Owl. Not because she has answers to all their questions, but because she can provide insight that will lead to questions that the two can spend a lifetime answering.

As Pouting Pig and Fixity Fox walk to the north edge of the Farm (an area as unfamiliar to Fixity Fox as the topic of spirituality), the setting sun radiates a purple glow across the sky. Fixity Fox mulls the day's events. Initially his plan was to get rid of Pouting Pig as soon as possible; yet somehow, he is actually enjoying the Pig's companionship. This being very unlike himself, Fixity Fox gathers that he must be getting delirious from only having eaten berries the entire day, and that once he picked and plucked a plump roaster, he would soon be his usual self—full, content, and clear-thinking.

Yet, strangely, he is neither hungry nor satisfied with the idea of going back to his normal routine of searching for hens.

Fixity Fox pulls his research from his pocket, and Pouting Pig's list of problems falls to the ground. He smoothens out the crumpled list and is struck by the last item: "I feel so empty inside." Fixity Fox feels uncomfortable, but then brushes off the uneasy feeling as he puts the list back in his pocket and retrieves the research he collected on spirituality. Of all the animals on the farm, he assumes that the one he would be least able to fool with his newfound knowledge would be the Omniscient Owl. "Hmmm," murmurs Fixity Fox as he skims the material, "Soul… God… religion… karma… fulfillment… enlightenment… inner peace. These are complicated, but interesting, concepts. But, I think I know enough to impress the Owl."

Putting his research back into his pocket, Fixity Fox turns to Pouting Pig, "When we get to the Omniscient Owl, she will impart wisdom regarding your spirituality—or lack thereof."

"Okay, but I don't know if I can remember all that I've learned so far. I'm tired, and plus I'm getting hungry again! I'm having a great time, but can we talk about spirituality tomorrow?"

In a serious tone, Fixity Fox, remembering something from his research, replies, "Address your spirituality today, because we are not promised tomorrow." He continues, "And don't worry, what you learn on our last visit will feed, not your stomach, but your soul!"

"What's a soul?"

"It's what makes you happy," says Fixity Fox without much thought, "And it puts a smile on your face."

"I thought good relationships, fulfilling work, and a positive self-image made an animal happy. How does the soul do this as well?"

Fixity Fox, curious to know the true role of the soul himself, replies, "The Owl and I will tell you. Just be patient."

Upon reaching the north edge of the farm, Fixity Fox calls out for the Omniscient Owl, "Mr. Owl. I mean *Ms.* Owl! We would like to speak to you!"

To get some rest, Pouting Pig stays back as Fixity Fox searches the trees that line the farm. As Pouting Pig lays on his back watching the fading light, he hears from above, "Hello, my friend. I take it that you are looking for me?"

Startled, Pouting Pig looks up to see Omniscient Owl above him. "Yes! Hello, Ms. Owl. Mr. Fox said that you could talk to me about my spirituality because I don't have any."

"Interesting. And is someone going to talk to Mr. Fox about his lack of spirituality?"

"Oh no, Mr. Fox is an expert on the subject, he knows about everything."

"I see," says Omniscient Owl. "I have been watching the two of you today, and I trust that both you and Mr. Fox have learned much. Now you want to know about spirituality. What an admirable goal! Let me begin by asking: What makes you think you have no spirituality?"

"I don't know what spirituality is, but Mr. Fox tells me I don't have any—so I guess I don't."

At this moment, Fixity Fox joins the two and says, "Finally, I have found you, Ms. Owl! And what is it Pig says I told him he doesn't have?"

Before Pouting Pig can answer, Omniscient Owl says, "Mr. Fox, it was not you who found me, but it was I who found the two of you. And Pouting Pig tells me that you told him that he has no spirituality. How is it that you've discerned this?"

"Well, Pig says that he's not happy and that he's got no motivation; therefore, I concluded that he has insufficient spirituality."

"Fox, are you happy? Do you have motivation?"

"Of course. I'm very pleased with myself, and I may be the most motivated animal on the farm. Besides you, of course," Fixity Fox quickly adds.

"Then, by your definition, you're very spiritual?"

"Sure I am."

"On what do you base your spirituality?"

Fixity Fox, stumped for an answer, replies a bit uncertainly, "Ms. Owl, I understand the nature of your questions; but this exercise is not about me. I'm not in need of fixing—Pig is."

Regaining his composure, Fixity Fox continues, "I know enough about the topic from what I've read in books to help Pig, but I'm sure he's tired of hearing me talk. So, I think it best if he learned about spirituality from you."

"I see," says Omniscient Owl. Then, addressing both Fixity Fox and Pouting Pig, she says, "To begin, one does not learn all they need to know about spirituality by reading a couple of books—or by talking to me for that matter. The quest for understanding one's spirituality and harnessing the power in one's soul can last a lifetime. By talking to you this evening, my only purpose is to open your mind to different ideas that you may wish to pursue further. And, Mr. Fox, by the end of our discussion, you may realize that you are not in a position to gauge another animal's level of spirituality before you gauge your own. To begin the discussion on spirituality, let me ask each of you: What do you believe in?"

"What do you mean?" Fixity Fox asks before Pouting Pig can speak.

"Do you believe in God or another deity, who made all animals? Do you believe in life after death? Do you believe that all animals have souls? Do you believe in a set of guiding principles that define right and wrong?"

Fixity Fox and Pouting Pig look at each other with confusion. After a moment of silence, Fixity Fox speaks first, "Those are a lot of questions, Omniscient Owl. I don't know how to answer them."

"I don't either," adds Pouting Pig.

"Let's take this slowly. Do you have faith?" Omniscient Owl asks.

"Faith in what? I have faith in myself," replies Fixity Fox.

"Having faith in one's self is easy. But do you have faith in things beyond yourself? Faith in that which you cannot control? In that which you cannot see?"

"I'm still not sure I understand," replies Fixity Fox, becoming frustrated that he was not able to grasp the points Omniscient Owl was trying to make.

"It may be that you do not understand because you have not defined that in which you believe, Mr. Fox."

"That's not true. I know what I believe in. I believe in money. I believe in every animal for himself. I believe that God helps those that help themselves." As soon as he says this last statement, Fox thinks, annoyed at himself, "I'm beginning to use slogans like Confident Cat!"

"Good, we're getting somewhere. You believe in things that you can control. However, do you believe in a greater power? Whatever that power may be?" Omniscient Owl asks as Fixity Fox and Pouting Pig listen intently. "Our first principle of Spirituality is—**Principle #21: Believe in things outside of your physical self.** Mark my words: we're not alone in this world. Forces, outside our sphere of influence, are all around us. Sometimes we can 'see' these forces, but more often than not, these forces are invisible to us."

"You see," continues Omniscient Owl, "It is very easy to have faith in the things that we know—that we are physically capable of. In fact, I overheard the conversation you had with Confident Cat, and he has a great amount of faith in his physical abilities. But that does not make him spiritual. Spirituality involves faith in your spiritual self: your Spirit, your Will, your Soul. Also, it includes faith in things greater than ourselves—things that we cannot see, hear, or touch; things that control and influence our destiny and our actions."

Fixity Fox and Pouting Pig exchange pensive looks as Omniscient Owl continues. "Additionally, spirituality involves those forces and concepts that are typically and inherently good and positive. Such as compassion for your fellow animal, or forgiveness, or even a stewardship of nature and the planet on which we live. Now, based on this definition, what do you believe in?"

After a moment, a perplexed Fixity Fox confesses, "I don't know. I've never given the concepts you mentioned much thought."

"What about you, Mr. Pig?" queries Omniscient Owl.

"I believe good pigs go to heaven. That's what my mother told me."

"Good, that constitutes a belief. Now, once you understand that spirituality is outside of our physical selves, the next principle of spirituality is—**Principle #22: Define what you believe in**. It is difficult to explore spirituality if you do not have grounding in your beliefs. And keep in mind: what you believe may change over time as you grow spiritually and as you learn more aspects of spirituality."

"Initially, most of us, like Pouting Pig, are told what to believe—for example, our parents and family define our beliefs. This is understandable, because when we are young, we don't have the capability nor the mental and spiritual capacity to define something as esoteric as belief."

Fixity Fox writes furiously as he attempts to capture all of what Omniscient Owl is saying.

Omniscient Owl continues, "As we get older and learn new things, we open our minds to other interpretations of belief. Based on this new information, we may either strengthen our existing beliefs, or we may modify our beliefs. We may be introduced to a concept that we've not heard before. We may feel that we've been 'enlightened.' In some cases, we may become disenchanted with what we once believed and reject it in favor of another belief. But whatever happens, I would like to stress the next principle—**Principle #23: Understand that one belief is not more "right" than another**—as long as the belief is a positive one, and not harmful to the self or others."

Fixity Fox asks, "If no belief is better than another, why is there such turmoil and conflict in the world over different beliefs?"

Omniscient Owl replies, "In my opinion, those who criticize another's beliefs are themselves violating one of the core tenets of spirituality: the acceptance of others and their ideas. Think about it this way: billions of animals live on this earth, so does it make sense for us all to have the same beliefs? After all, we all have different cultures, speak different languages, eat different foods, and experience life differently. Therefore, a logical and truly spiritual person should accept that spiritual beliefs and concepts of spirituality will differ as well."

"Having said that, another principle of spirituality is ensuring that once you decide on a belief—**Principle #24: Act in accordance with your belief**. For example, if your belief is based on showing love to your fellow animals, then do that. Don't harm and belittle others. Make sure you accept others. Be inclusive, not exclusive. As our friend Confident Cat would say, make sure you 'practice what you preach.' And as Conscience Cat mentioned in your conversation, this is where one's conscience comes into play. Your spirituality can help inform your conscience to help you define what's right and wrong. Pouting Pig, how do you define right and wrong?"

"Right things are things that I do that help other animals. Wrong things are things that hurt other animals. I make sure I don't do these things."

"Good answer, Pouting Pig. Mr. Fox, how do you define right and wrong?"

"Right and wrong?" Fixity Fox pauses and then replies, "To be honest Ms. Owl, I've never really defined things in my life in terms of right and wrong."

"Then what keeps you from doing things that you should not do?"

"I'm not sure. I do what I need to do to survive and to ensure that my needs are taken care of."

"Even at the expense of others? What about the needs of other animals?"

Becoming agitated with Omniscient Owl's questions, and his own insufficient answers, Fixity Fox responds combatively, "Deciding what's good and what's bad is not as simple as Pig's answer seems. The reality is, to make it in this world, animals have to live by their instincts—and it's a clear matter of survival of the fittest! Further, who says that I should also be responsible for ensuring that other animals are taken care of? Why should this be my responsibility? Frankly, it's not in my best interest to help others. Every animal should be able to take care of themselves! And if they can't, that's their tough luck!"

Fixity Fox begins to feel uneasy when Omniscient Owl doesn't immediately reply, and as he realizes the impact of what he has said. After a moment of uncomfortable silence, Pouting Pig tugs at Fixity Fox's jacket with tears in his eyes, "Mr. Fox, if you feel this way, why are you helping me?"

Fixity Fox looks down at the sad Pouting Pig and feels a painful twinge in his chest. He realizes that he has hurt Pouting Pig's feelings, and has belittled him and his thoughts all during the day's journey.

At this point, Omniscient Owl speaks again, "Let me tell you a story about what happened at the last farm I lived near."

Am I My Brother's Keeper?

A mouse looked through the crack in the wall to see the farmer's wife opening a package. "What food might this contain?" The mouse asks. He was devastated to discover it was a mousetrap. Retreating to the farmyard, the mouse proclaimed the warning. "There is a mousetrap in the house! There is a mousetrap in the house!"

The chicken clucked and scratched, raised her head and said, "Mr. Mouse, I can tell this is a grave concern to you, but it is of no consequence to me. I cannot be bothered by it."

The mouse turned to the goat, and the goat said, "I am so very sorry, Mr. Mouse, but there is nothing I can do about it but pray. Be assured that you are in my prayers."

The mouse turned to the cow who said, "Wow, Mr. Mouse. I'm sorry for you. But it's no skin off my nose." So the mouse returned to the house, head down and dejected, to face the farmer's mousetrap alone. That very night, a sound was heard throughout the house like the sound of a mousetrap catching its prey. The farmer's wife rushed to see what was caught, and in the darkness she did not see that it was a venomous snake whose tail the trap had caught. When the wife got close to the trap, the snake bit her.

The farmer rushed his wife to the hospital, and she returned home with a fever. Now everyone knows you treat a fever with fresh chicken soup, so the farmer went to the farmyard for the soup's main ingredient. But his wife's sickness continued, so friends came to sit with her around the clock. To feed them, the farmer butchered the goat.

The farmer's wife did not get well, and she died. So many people came to her funeral that the farmer had the cow slaughtered to provide enough meat for all of them.

—Author Unknown

Omniscient Owl stops speaking and removes her glasses and puts them in her pocket. Fixity Fox thinks about the story and his own hurtful comments. He has always prided himself in not needing anyone, and he has never felt the need to help another animal without some gain for himself. But he realized more, now than ever, that he did have something in common with Pouting Pig—an empty feeling inside. His world has always revolved around himself; he has never considered the concept of a greater power existing in the world, or the idea that all animals were put on earth to ensure the well-being of other animals. For the first time, Fixity Fox wonders if learning more about spirituality and practicing its concepts could fill the void he had inside. In fact, as the day has progressed, he has obtained a sense of well-being as Pouting Pig's attitude improved. Could using his knowledge to help others also increase his spirituality?

Fixity Fox looks to Omniscient Owl and then back to Pouting Pig, clears his throat, and responds to Pouting Pig's earlier question, "Pouting Pig, I have a confession to make. When I first decided to help you, my plan was to trick you into thinking I had helped you so I could obtain something I wanted. But, as we met with the animals today, I began to enjoy our time together and the fact that I might be helping you. I also realize that many areas of my own life need fixing. In fact, I'm not sure what my own purpose in life is. Please forgive me, Pig, for thinking I was better than you, and for trying to deceive you." When he finishes talking, Fixity Fox lowers his head again as he takes off his Fixity Fox name tag, crumples it, and throws it on the ground.

"But, Mr. Fox, you have helped me! I have really learned a lot, and I'm not sad anymore."

Omniscient Owl responds, "Thank you for your honesty, Mr. Fox. Becoming spiritual can begin with recognizing that we are not perfect, acknowledging our failings, and having a desire to look beyond ourselves for a meaning and purpose in life. Also, having a healthy spirituality can help improve your other Life Aspects—such as your self-perception and your relationships."

Omniscient Owl continues, "If you or young Pig decide that spirituality is something you feel should be important to you, and you decide to embark on an effort to define your spirituality, remember what I said at the beginning of our conversation: Becoming spiritual is not a one-time activity. Animals devoted to their spirituality can spend their entire lives strengthening it. So our last principle is—**Principle #25: Continually strengthen your spirituality**."

Fixity Fox writes this principle down and says, "Thank you, Ms. Owl, for your insight. I truly appreciate you sharing with us. You're right about so many things."

Omniscient Owl flies down from the tree limb, picks up the crumpled name tag Fixity Fox had thrown aside, and gives it back to him, saying, "Mr. Fox, spirituality is not a matter of *being* right. It's a matter of *feeling* and *doing* right."

"Make sure you write that down, Mr. Fox," Pouting Pig jokes.

"Yes, sir, Mr. Pig," responds Fixity Fox, laughing.

After saying their goodbyes, Fixity Fox walks Pouting Pig back to the barn. "Pig, get some rest," says Fixity Fox. "Tomorrow we will apply what we have learned and perform the rest of the Life Improvement Methodology. Come to my den at 1:00 p.m."

"Thanks for helping me, Mr. Fox!" Pouting Pig says, hugging Fixity Fox.

"Thank you, Pig, for helping me as well. And from now on, call me Fixity," he says as he turns to walk back to his lonely den.

Once home, Fixity Fox looks over his notes and reviews the day's events in his mind to figure out how he was going to use this information to help Pouting Pig find his purpose. And just as important, he realizes he needs to understand his own purpose as well. Fixity Fox ponders this as he paces back and forth in his den. After hours of fruitless thought, he goes to bed, where he tosses and turns, still frustrated that he didn't know what the purpose of his life was. Finally, the frustrated Fixity Fox falls asleep.

While sleeping, Fixity Fox has a dream. In the dream, he is on his way to the hen house on a day that both the Farmer and the Lovable Lab would be gone for the entire day. Therefore, he would have his pick of as many hens as he wanted. As he is about to enter the unguarded hen house, he hears the crying of Pouting Pig. Fixity Fox turns and sees the despondent Pig standing on the bank of the swimming pond with a big brick tied around one of his legs. Pouting Pig cries out, "Goodbye cruel world!"

Fixity Fox pauses and considers his options: Gather as many hens as his arms could carry, or save the poor Pig? Fox surprises himself by turning and rushing toward the pond to save Pouting Pig just as he was going to jump in the pond. For some reason, Fixity Fox felt it was more **important** to help Pouting Pig than to satiate his gluttonous hunger. Fixity Fox is further surprised by the feeling of **satisfaction** he feels after talking Pouting Pig into taking the brick off his leg and then cheering him up. Fixity Fox wonders that if it was satisfying to fix one animal, what if he fixed many animals?

Inspired by his dream, Fixity Fox jumps out of bed and writes down some thoughts for the next day. He goes back to sleep feeling that he had begun to solve the mystery of finding one's purpose.

Fixity Fox's Life Principles—Spirituality

(Provided Graciously by the Omniscient Owl)

- Principle #21: Believe in Things Outside of Your Physical Self.
- Principle #22: Define What You Believe In.
- Principle #23: Understand That One Belief is Not More "Right" Than Another.
- Principle #24: Act In Accordance to Your Belief.
- Principle #25: Continually Strengthen Your Spirituality.

(Note: Fixity Fox will provide additional information in Chapter 8 regarding specific actions related to these principles.)

Reader Reflection:

Do you consider yourself a spiritual person? If not, is it because you've made a conscious decision not to be, or is it because, like Fixity Fox, you've not given the concept much thought? Often, we are so busy living our lives and ensuring that our tangible needs are met that we don't think about the intangibles, or how we fit into the bigger picture, e.g., our role on this planet.

If you are spiritual, how did you define your beliefs? Were they defined for you, like was the case with Pouting Pig? Or did you embark on a quest to define your own spirituality? Or, did you experience a turning point in your life when you suddenly felt the power of spirituality?

Of all the Life Aspects, spirituality is the most personal, and many times, the most contentious and debated. This is due to the personal and strong nature of "beliefs." **Assignment 1:** Conduct research on a belief other than yours. What are the major differences you found; what were the similarities? Do you agree with the belief you researched? Do you feel the belief is a valid one?

The Owl was located at the North edge of the farm—what is your "True North"—those beliefs that act as your guiding compass? Here are some additional questions to ponder:

- *Are you religious, spiritual, or both? Is there a difference between the two? If so, what? Can someone be spiritual without believing in a higher Being?*
- *Are you tolerant of beliefs that are different than yours? Are you accepting of individuals that may be different from the mainstream? If not, is this in accordance with your spirituality?*
- *Do you know individuals or groups that profess to be spiritual, yet their actions indicate otherwise? Does this make them less spiritual? How does their behavior make you feel? Do you practice what you preach?*
- *Can a person be a truly "good" person without being spiritual or religious?*

Assignment 2: Take time to think about these questions; get a group together and discuss them. When you're ready—back to the story!

Chapter 6: Conduct Your Assessment

What's important to me, what do I need to fix?
Take an honest assessment and see.
Answer the statements honestly, and get your results;
The answer is where your purpose may be!

At 1:00 p.m. Pouting Pig knocks on Fixity Fox's door, who comes out with an armful of paper.

"Hello, Mr. Fox—I mean Fixity. I'm glad you wanted to see me today because I did a lot of thinking, and I really need help understanding how I'm supposed to use all of the information that you gave me yesterday."

"Good morning," says Fixity Fox. "It's good to see you, too. Now, hold that thought and make yourself comfortable while I set up shop." Fixity Fox gives Pouting Pig an apple and tacks a piece of paper with the Life Aspect Model drawn on it, to a tree.

Once satisfied with the placement of his materials, Fixity Fox turns to Pouting Pig, "I appreciate your participation yesterday. The objective of our trip was to give you an understanding of the Life Aspects Model." Fixity Fox points to the circle on the tree.

"The pie!" Pouting Pig shouts. "Can I find my purpose based on that?"

"You sure can."

"It's a ***Purpose Pie*** then! A ***Purpose Pie***!" Pouting Pig exclaims.

Deciding not to counter Pouting Pig's suggestion, Fixity Fox responds, "Okay, fine—we'll call it a Purpose Pie. Now, before we begin today, do you have any questions?"

"Yes," replies Pouting Pig, anxious to talk. "I really liked listening to each of the animals yesterday, but what do I do with all that information? How do I use it to improve my life? What about all of those Life Principles? Do I have to work on all those things at once?"

Addressing Pouting Pig's multiple questions, Fixity Fox responds, "Of course not. And, it *is* a wealth of information to digest, and yes, you may have a lot to work on, but not everything we learned will apply to you. Remember what I told you when we began this adventure? You will need to *Prioritize*."

"That's right, I remember, *Prioritize*," repeats Pouting Pig, glad that he remembered the word from yesterday. "But how do I prioritize? I don't even know where to start!"

"This is a good segue into what I want to teach you next. We're going to conduct an assessment of your life in terms of each of the four Life Aspects. This constitutes *Step 2* of the methodology I showed you yesterday," says Fixity Fox as he tacks the Life Improvement Methodology graphic on the tree:

“To conduct this assessment, you’ll need to complete a Life Improvement Assessment Questionnaire, or in layman’s terms, a survey of sorts. The survey contains a number of statements, and each statement corresponds to one of the four Life Aspects. You’ll be asked how important each statement is to you, and also how satisfied you are with your life in terms of each statement.” Fixity Fox retrieves the assessment questionnaire he spent all morning developing.

“You’ve used this survey many times before?”

Fixity Fox, about to lie, instead replies, “I am pleased to let you know you will be the very first one to take the survey.”

Fixity Fox continues, “Based on how you answer the statements, the survey will accomplish three things:”

(1) “Identify the importance of each of your Life Aspects,

(2) “Calculate how satisfied you are with each Life Aspect in your current life, and

(3) “Identify improvement areas.”

“The statements on the survey are derived in part from the discussions we had yesterday, and in part from in-depth psychological and scientif—” Fixity Fox stops. “Well, in part from some research I conducted. Do you have any questions?”

“I’m excited; I’m ready to take the survey,” Pouting Pig replies as he tries to grab one of the surveys from Fixity Fox’s hands.

“Hold your horses, little one. When you get the survey, read the instructions and remember to answer the statements as honestly as possible.” Fixity Fox hands Pouting Pig the survey and a Number 2 pencil.

Pouting Pig takes the survey, looks at the format and frowns. “This looks like a test. What if I answer something wrong?”

“It’s not a test, and fret not, there are no wrong answers, Pig. Answer the questions based on how you feel.”

As Pouting Pig begins to take the survey, Fixity Fox decides to take it as well, interested in what his results would say about his own life.

Note to the Reader:

It's now time for **you** to take the Pout or Purpose Assessment Survey.

The survey can be found at the following website:

http://www.poutorpurpose.com

Click on the link to take the survey. That's right, no Number 2 pencils needed! Answer the questions as honestly as possible based on how you feel each statement relates to your current life. For example, answer the importance statements based on how important you feel the statements **are** in your life currently, not based on how important you feel these statements **should be** in your life.

After taking the survey, print your completed survey form and your results so you can easily refer to these during the rest of the chapter, which focuses on interpreting the results. When you're done with the survey, let's go back to the story!

(**Note:** for readers that do not have access to the Internet, please send a self addressed, stamped envelop to K.C. Fox Publishing at the address on the copyright page, and we'll send you a survey form in the mail.)

After some time has passed, Pouting Pig throws his hands in the air and exclaims, "There! I'm done. Fixity, I'm done with my survey. What do I do now? How do I fix myself?"

Fixity Fox finishes his own survey and replies, "Let me score your survey so we can review the results together. Relax for a few minutes while I do this." Fixity Fox takes the survey from Pouting Pig and pulls a calculator from his pocket to tabulate Pouting Pig's results as well as his own. While he waits, Pouting Pig munches happily on his apple.

After much calculation and recalculation, Fixity Fox says, "Okay, I'm done, Pig," as he hands Pouting Pig his results.

Pouting Pig glances at the sheets of paper and exclaims, "Wow, this is a lot of information, and these are pretty charts and graphs. But what does it all mean?"

"That's what we'll talk about next," Fixity Fox responds as he collects his notes. "Your survey results are presented in six sections. Let's start with the first section."

Note to the Reader:

To interpret your results, please have your results handy, and follow along with the rest of the chapter. Note: Reading the remainder of the chapter without your results will not be as beneficial to you!

<u>Results Section 1: Importance Ranking</u>

"For each statement on the survey," explains Fixity Fox, "You were asked how important that statement is to you. The importance score for all statements was averaged by Life Aspect, and the results identify which Life Aspects are most important to you. The first part of the importance results tell you which of the animals we talked to yesterday you most resemble. Look at your results and see what animal you are."

Fixity Fox gives Pouting Pig a second to read this result before continuing.

"Let me give you a description of each of the animals," says Fixity Fox as he hands Pouting Pig a sheet of paper with information about each animal.

Animals and Life Aspects

Lovable Lab (Life Aspect—Relationships)

- Personality: Desires strong relationships. Typically extroverted and very protective of others.
- Likes: Spending time with others; bonding; emoting; talking; and listening.
- Dislikes: Conflict; hurting others' feelings; feeling alone.

Hardworking Horse (Life Aspect—Career)

- Personality: Places a fair amount of emphasis on work. Strives to do a very good job. Can define themselves based on the type of work they do.
- Likes: Successfully completing a work-related project; receiving recognition for work well done; earning a job title that conveys success.
- Dislikes: Undefined job or project objectives; distractions that get in the way of finishing work; retirement or downtime. Very little patience for those who don't do good work.

Centered Cat (Life Aspect—Self)

- Personality: Places a fair amount of emphasis on improving their physical fitness, mental fitness, financial stability, and/or creativity. Sometimes feel that they cannot love others until they love themselves. Can be focused on how the world sees them.
- Likes: Achieving; succeeding; creating; learning; competing; setting goals; receiving recognition for being good at something.
- Dislikes: Self-failure; individuals without goals; having a feeling of not making a difference.

Omniscient Owl (Life Aspect—Spirituality)

- Personality: Tends to view the world based on spiritual beliefs.
- Likes: Being close to their deity; enriching their knowledge of beliefs; discussing beliefs with others; performing good deeds.
- Dislikes: Ambiguity in their beliefs, or when their beliefs are challenged or disproved. Sometimes dislikes those with dissimilar beliefs.

Fixity Fox lets Pouting Pig review the information and continues, "The second part of the importance ranking provides a bar chart that ranks the Life Aspects in terms of how important you ranked them on a scale from 0%-100%. The higher the score, the more important the aspect in your life. Pig, take a look at you results, and then let me show you these examples."

Example Importance Rankings

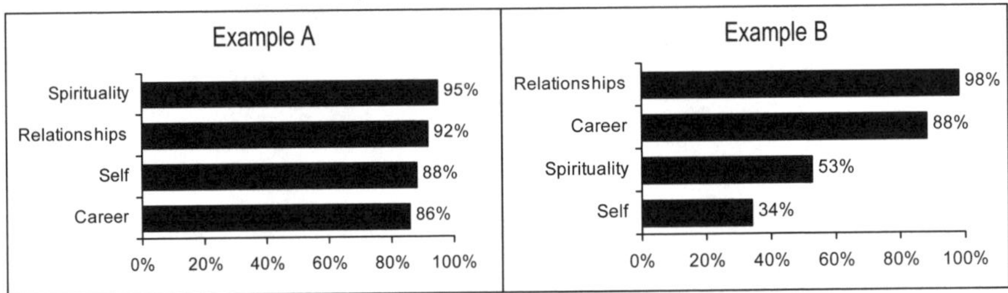

"In both examples, the Life Aspect that is most important is placed at the top of the chart, followed in descending order by the other Life Aspects. In Example A, the importance rankings are close to each other, meaning they are all important to the individual, but the individual's dominant type is Omniscient Owl (95%), followed closely by Lovable Lab (92%). In Example B, there's a clear delineation of importance, as this individual is clearly a Lovable Lab (98%) and doesn't place much importance on the Self Life Aspect (34%)."

Fixity Fox pauses a moment, then asks. "Based on these examples, which animal would you say is in better shape than the other?"

Pouting Pig looks at the two examples and frowns in thought, and then seeing something, he exclaims, "The animal in the first example!"

"And why would that be?"

"Because the bars are bigger and closer together."

"That's an understandable conclusion, one that many may draw. However, the importance rankings are all individual in nature, thus, one is not better than another. Let's discuss how these importance ranking examples translate into the next results."

Pouting Pig reviews his own satisfaction scores and asks, "What's a good satisfaction score?"

Looking at his notes, Fixity Fox responds, "For simplicity's sake, I like to use the scale teachers use in school—a percentage score in the 90s would receive a grade of an A; a score in the 80s a B; in the 70s a C; in the 60s a D; and anything below that would be an F."

Pouting Pig replies, "Anytime I bring home a grade lower than a B from my school, my mother says I need to work on that subject. So does that mean everything on my results that scored lower than 80% is something I need to work on?"

"Not quite. A low satisfaction score does not necessarily mean you need to work on an item. For example, assume you got a grade of C- in a class that is part of an important course of study that you need to graduate from school. I would say that you need to improve in that subject so that you don't continue to receive low grades in this course of study. However, let's assume that you received the same grade in a class that was not needed for graduation, and was not as important to your course of study. Your need to improve your skills in this area therefore, isn't as important. This is where the 'Importance Rankings' I will explain later are taken into account."

Fixity Fox continues, "Now, let's look again at an example pie chart, but this time as it relates to satisfaction results."

Results Section 4: Satisfaction Proportion Chart

"The next pie graph divides your Purpose Pie into your proportions of satisfaction. The larger a Life Aspect's pie piece, the greater the share of satisfaction with this Life Aspect in your life."

Example Satisfaction Proportion Chart

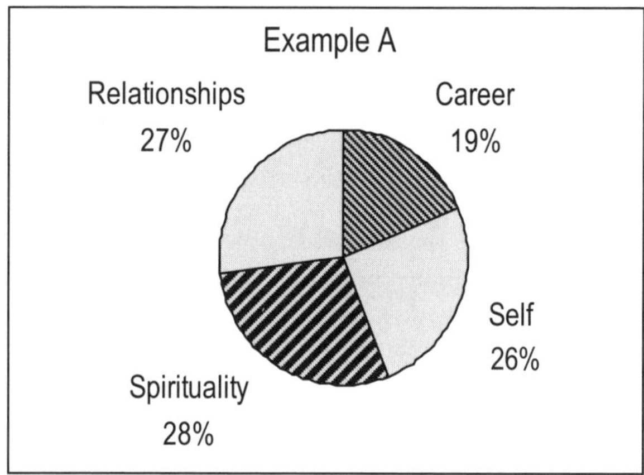

"This example shows an animal who's most satisfied with his or her spirituality and least satisfied with his or her career. Once again, the slices of everyone's pies will vary based on their level of satisfaction. Some pies will have slices nearly all the same size, and others will have pies with different size pieces. And as I explained earlier, since the pie chart is based on proportions, a large slice doesn't necessarily mean that you are *very* satisfied with an aspect, instead it indicates that you are *more* satisfied with that aspect in comparison to the others." Fixity Fox lets Pouting Pig review his results in this section and then continues.

Results Section 5: Improvement Ranking by Life Aspect

"Pig, following up to a question you had earlier about what areas you should improve, let's now talk about the results that depict the Life Aspects that need improving."

"To calculate the Improvement Rankings, I analyzed each statement based on how important it was to you **and** how satisfied you are with it. Remember: You may be dissatisfied with something, but if it's not important to you, then you may not need to improve it. Let's look at an example."

Example Improvement Ranking

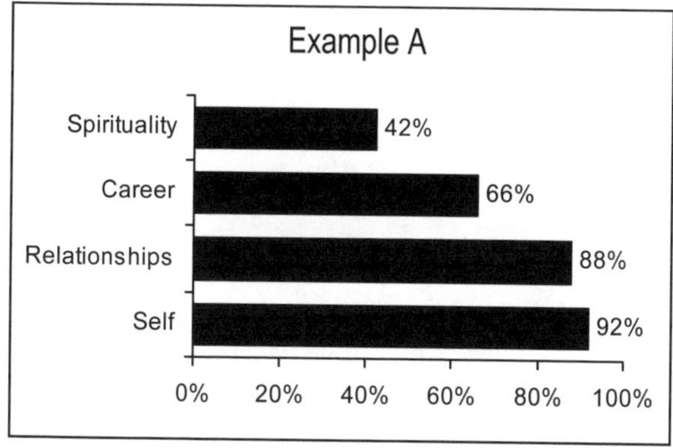

"One of the first things you'll notice about your results, and the example above, is that the Life Aspects are ranked in ascending order."

"Ascending order?" Pouting Pig asks.

"From smallest to largest."

"Thank you, Fixity, I'm learning so much from you," says Pouting Pig as he writes the definition of the word.

"My pleasure," replies Fixity Fox, genuinely liking the satisfaction he is obtaining from teaching. "The chart is in ascending order because those items that scored the lowest are the items that need the most improvement, thus, the items you should focus on first."

"I also want you to look at your results in this section and compare them to the list of problems you wrote when we started your journey," says Fixity Fox as he hands Pouting Pig the once crumpled list of problems. "Take some time to determine if the majority of the problems you wrote are related to your lowest, and second lowest Life Aspect. Typically this is the case."

As Pouting Pig looks at his results, Fixity Fox assesses his own.

"How do I improve something that scored low?" Pouting Pig asks after some time.

"Hold that thought. And let's look at the last category of results first; then I will explain the steps to take for improvement."

Results Section 6: Improvement Rankings by Statement

"So far, I have given you many results to digest, and you have asked numerous times how you go about improving your life. The final section of results helps point you in the correct direction. If you look at your results, you'll see that the survey statements are grouped into the following Action Categories:

- *"Immediate Improvement Needed:* These statements scored the lowest.
- *"Some Improvement Needed*: These statements received an average grade.
- *"Almost There*: These statements received a fairly good grade.
- *"Great Shape*: These statements scored the highest."

(Note to the Reader: Your results will only have the categories in which your statements scored.)

Fixity Fox continues, "Your survey statements are grouped in the order they need improving—the first statement needs the most improvement; the last statement needs the least."

"Will all of the statements that I score low on relate to the Life Aspect that scored the lowest in my Improvement Rankings by Life Aspect?" Pouting Pig asks.

"Excellent question! Many of the lowest scoring statements will relate to the Life Aspect that scored the lowest in your Section 5 Improvement Rankings by Life Aspect, however, not all of them do, because the Life Aspect scoring is based on the ***average*** score of all the statements for that Life Aspect. Therefore, some statements can be scored high and some can be scored low."

Fixity Fox continues, "Take some time to review how your statements scored and compare your low scoring statements to your original problem list while I get ready for our next exercise."

Pouting Pig looks at his statements as Fixity Fox begins preparing to discuss the next topic. After looking at all his results, Pouting Pig thinks about everything that was bothering him the day before and tries to draw a connection between his problems and what to do next.

Note to the Reader:

Take some time to reflect on your own results. Look at your lowest scoring statements in Section 6 of your results. Do you agree that these areas need the most improvement? Were there any surprises on your results?

What unanswered questions do you still have? Let's see if our friend Fixity Fox has the answer to some of them.

Now back to the story…

After a few moments of silence, Pouting Pig says, "Okay Fixity, I've reviewed my results and I've been really listening to everything you've said, honestly I have, but…" he trails off unsure of how to express his feelings.

"Go ahead, Pig, spit it out."

"I don't feel fixed yet!" replies a frustrated Pouting Pig. "Shouldn't I feel different now that I have all my results? Also, just because I know what items I need to improve, and even if I know what my Purpose Pie looks like, **how does this tell me what my purpose is?**"

"Another excellent question," replies Fixity Fox with a twinkle in his eye remembering his dream from the night before. "I'm just about to tell you. It's fairly simple…"

Fixity Fox's Assessment Guidelines

- There are no right or wrong answers to the survey statements, and there are no right or wrong results.
- Answer the statements based on how you feel or live your life today.
- Just because you are dissatisfied with something doesn't mean you need to improve it.
- The largest slice of your Purpose Pie is typically where your purpose can be found—your survey results and your Purpose Pie are used to identify this purpose!

Reader Reflection:

Were you surprised by any of the results? In the Section 1 results, what animal from the book were you? Do you see characteristics of yourself similar to how the animal was depicted in the book? Look at your Purpose Pie from Section 2—do your pie slice percentages reflect how you spend your time? Also, in a given week, do you spend an adequate percentage of your time on your most important Life Aspect?

In Section 3, what Life Aspect are you most satisfied with? Look again at the Life Aspect from Section 1 that you found most important. Are these two Life Aspects the same? Surprisingly, most often these two Life Aspects are different. This happens because there are things in our lives that are important to us, yet, due to circumstances, we're not satisfied with our lives in this area. **Assignment 1:** If your top Life Aspect from Section 1 (Importance) differed from the top Life Aspect in Section 3 (Satisfaction), ask yourself, "Why?" What's getting in the way of you being satisfied with your most important Life Aspect?

In Section 5, which Life Aspects need the most improvement? For many people who took the test version of the survey, this was the same Life Aspect that was most important to them. **Assignment 2:** Refer to your problems that you wrote when you began the book. Do items on your list correspond to your top two Life Aspects that need improvement?

In Section 6, how many items were in the category "Immediate Improvement Needed"? Of the four categories, which category had the most items in it? Once again, do any of the statements in the two lowest categories correspond to the list of problems you wrote? Did you find that some of the items on your list of problems did not need immediate improvement compared to other more pressing problems?

Are you still wondering how all of this information can be used to help you identify your purpose? If so, let's get back to the story.

Chapter 7: Understanding Your Purpose

How do I know what to do with my life?
I know what's wrong now, but what should I do?
In answer to your question, it's fairly simple,
Do what's important ***and*** *satisfying to you!*

Reflecting back on his dream from the night before, Fixity Fox replies to Pouting Pig's question about identifying his purpose, "Pig, you've asked an important question, the answer to which is not as complex as you would think. To understand your purpose:

"Determine what's important to you,
Make sure you're satisfied with what's important to you, and
Do what's important to you."

Fixity Fox lets this sink in and continues, "Some animals spend their lives agonizing about their purpose and how they should go about finding it. Many times, they over-analyze this concept of 'purpose,' when it can be rather simple. Let me explain what I mean. Based on your results, let's say that the spirituality slice is the largest slice on your Purpose Pie in terms of importance. Therefore, it's safe to assume that your purpose will most likely be related to spirituality. Conversely, if the career Life Aspect is the least important to you, then your purpose probably will not be career-related."

Fixity Fox continues, "But it's hard to fulfill your purpose if you're not satisfied with what's important to you. Using the same example, if spirituality is most important to you, but you're not satisfied with your spirituality, it'll be hard for you to achieve your spirituality-related purpose until you improve your life in this area. Does this make sense?"

Pouting Pig thinks about this for a moment and replies, "Yes, I think I get it now."

"Good, now let's connect your results to your purpose. Look at your survey results related to importance (Sections 1 and 2). Which Life Aspect is most important to you? Now look at the Improvement Ranking by Statement section of your results (Section 6). Which statements related to this Life Aspect show up in the 'Needs Immediate Improvement' or 'Some Improvement Needed' categories, and which statements show up in the other categories? Also, look back at your completed survey form that I gave you; what statements did you mark as very important?"

Pouting Pig reviews his results and his completed survey form and after some time responds, "My self Life Aspect is the most important; however, in Section 6, I have four self-related statements that need immediate improvement. I also have a couple of relationship statements that need immediate improvement as well. And on my survey form, I rated, as very important, a couple statements related to helping others and making a difference."

"Okay, so you'll probably have a self-related purpose, along with something related to helping others. Using all this information together, can you think of a purpose for yourself?" Fixity Fox queries.

Pouting Pig thinks about this for a while. "I'm not sure. Could you give me an example of what someone's purpose could be?"

"Of course, take a look at this table that I drew that contains examples of purposes."

Purpose Table

Life Aspect	My Purpose in Life is to...	
■ Relationships	■ Raise a loving family ■ Enrich the lives of others	■ Be a good friend to others ■ Support those important to me
■ Career	■ Be seen as an expert in my field ■ Do work that benefits others	■ Attain a top position in my career field ■ Make a lot of money in my job
■ Self—Confidence, Physical	■ Be in top physical shape ■ Be as healthy as possible	■ Look as good as I can ■ Be very good in a certain sport ■ Help others be healthy
■ Self—Financial	■ Be wealthy ■ Own numerous properties	■ Accumulate assets that can be passed to my children ■ Earn money to help others
■ Self—Sensuality	■ Express my sensuality ■ Be sensual with others	■ Help others feel comfortable with their sensuality
■ Self—Mental	■ Be as smart as I can be ■ Educate others	■ Use my mental abilities to help solve problems that can help others
■ Self—Conscience	■ Help those that cannot help themselves ■ Protect the planet	■ Raise the awareness of others regarding important issues ■ Make the world a better place
■ Self—Creativity	■ Create art that pleases myself and others ■ Create art that has a message	■ Invent things that improve the standard of living ■ Engage in fulfilling hobbies
■ Spirituality	■ Inform others of my beliefs ■ Be enlightened ■ Serve God	■ Be good to my fellow man ■ Be saved ■ Make the world a better place

Fixity Fox continues, "As you can see, one's purpose can be very simple and touch a small number of others, or it can be a grand purpose and touch many. Neither type of purpose is better than the other (as long as the purpose is not a harmful one) because we're all different and have unique desires and needs."

"Also, your purpose can include characteristics of more than one Life Aspect. For example, you can paint masterpieces for your own satisfaction (Self), but you can do it also to convey a spiritual message to others (Spirituality). Or, you may want a fulfilling job (Career), where you can pursue your passion of bonding with neglected or special-needs children (Relationships)."

"Okay, that makes sense," says Pouting Pig. "But once I pick a purpose, am I allowed to change it later, or is that my purpose for the rest of my life?"

"Your purpose does not need to remain static, it can change over time based on where you are in your life. Remember—your purpose is based on what's important to you, and typically what's important to you changes over your lifetime. What's important to you as a young Piglet will most likely be different than what's important to you once you're an old hog."

Fixity Fox continues, "I now want you to look at your results, identify what's important to you, and then use this information to complete *Step 3* of the Life Improvement Methodology."

Life Improvement Methodology

"Your ***Purpose Statement*** is important because it serves as a tangible manifestation of what you feel is your purpose in life. It's a document that can be used to give your life direction. It's something you can refer to when you feel you're drifting off course."

Fixity Fox hands Pouting Pig a blank piece of paper and continues, "To get you started, create your Purpose Statement by completing this statement:

"My purpose in life is to...."

Pouting Pig looks at the statement then asks, "Does it matter how much I write?"

"No, your Purpose Statement can be as short or as long as you like."

Pouting Pig reviews his survey results, thinks for a few moments and then begins writing his Purpose Statement. After some time, and many changes, Pouting Pig shouts, "Fixity, I'm done! I think I know what I want my purpose to be!"

Fixity Fox takes the paper from Pouting Pig and reads it aloud:

"My purpose in life is to become as smart as I can so I can then use my smarts to make the world a better place. My purpose is to also have good relationships with those important to me."

"Is my Purpose Statement okay?" Pouting Pig asks.

"It sure is," replies Fixity Fox impressed with what Pouting Pig wrote.

"Good! So I'm fixed now, right?"

"Not quite. You have results from your survey, and you have a Purpose Statement; but having this information alone will not cause changes in your life because you have only part of the solution. The other part involves doing something with the information. It involves ***Taking Action***!" Fixity Fox exclaims as he strikes his pointer into the air for emphasis.

"Which brings us to the last step of our methodology—we will now create your own special ***Life Improvement Plan***."

Fixity Fox's Tips on Understanding Your Purpose

- Purpose is a manifestation of that which is important and satisfying to you.
- Purposes can be simple or grand, and one purpose is not better than another purpose (as long as the purpose is not harmful to others).
- A purpose can encompass more than one Life Aspect.
- Your purpose can change throughout your life.
- A Purpose Statement represents a roadmap to guide your life.
- Finding you purpose and acting on your results require taking action!

Reader Reflection:

Do you feel someone's purpose should be more complex than how it was described by Fixity Fox? If so, why? Some of the example Purpose Statements presented earlier may seem very self-focused. Do you feel that there's anything wrong with this? Or, do you feel that someone's purpose should be "good" and involve helping others?

Assignment 1: Look back at your purpose that you wrote at the end of Chapter 1 (you wrote one right?), and try to reword it into the Purpose Statement format. Will you change your purpose based on what you now know from the story?

Read your Purpose Statement out loud and think about this—can you live up to your Purpose Statement? Consider this: Most of my work as a consultant involves working with organizations. The corporate equivalent of a Purpose Statement is a corporate Mission Statement that states why the organization is in business and what it wants to achieve. A mission statement also serves as a guiding instrument for the organization and its employees. However, I've found that many organizations don't live up to what they've written in their Mission Statement because the concepts written aren't reflected in the way the organization actually conducts business. The same can happen with a personal Purpose Statement. To avoid this, strive to ensure that once you put your statement into practice, you are able to identify the connection between what you've written and your deeds and actions.

Assignment 2 (Optional): When you are finished writing your Purpose Statement, you can post it on the *Pout or Purpose?* website and also review other reader's statements.

Are you ready to take action related to your purpose and improving your Life Aspects? If so, on with the story…

Chapter 8: Develop Your Life Improvement Plan

You have a Purpose Statement and survey results, what to do next?
Take action by creating a Life Improvement Plan!
"I'll create a plan, but will it really make a difference?"
Hear me when I say this—"Sure it can!"

"Okay, Pig, we now arrive at the culmination of our journey—where the rubber hits the road. Research shows that many improvement efforts undertaken by organizations and individuals fail because the results are not acted on. Either the organizations or individuals don't know how to act on the results, or they don't have the fortitude to make the needed changes. The long and short of it is, results without action do not amount to much."

"I have the fortitude! Or at least I think I do," replies Pouting Pig.

"Good! It's now time for us to determine what to do based on the results of your assessment. And what we decide will be used to create your personalized Life Improvement Plan—as indicated in the final step of our Life Improvement Methodology."

Life Improvement Methodology

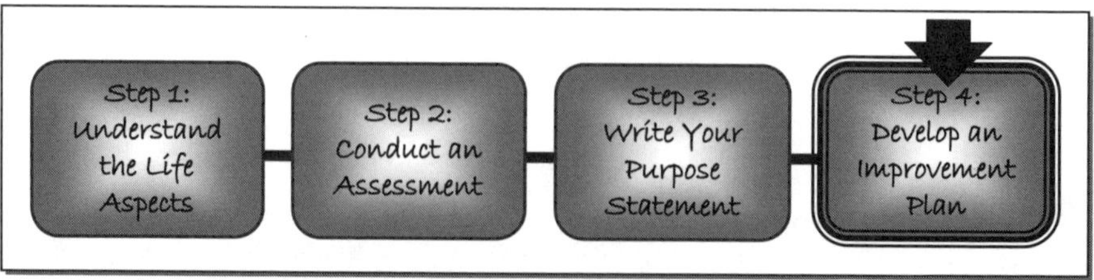

"To decide what you should include on your improvement plan, we will conduct four activities. Let's begin with the first one."

Activity 1: Identify What to Improve

"Begin by looking at your Purpose Statement and identifying what you need to improve in order to accomplish what you've written. This can be done by looking at which Life Improvement Aspects need improving."

Fixity Fox continues, "How does one improve an overall Life Aspect you may ask? I suggest we refer to the Life Improvement Principles we captured yesterday and then determine which of the principles on the list you could improve. To assist in conducting this activity, I have conveniently summarized all of the Life Improvement Principles by Life Aspect in a useful manner for you."

Note to the Reader:

All 25 Life Improvement Principles are summarized on the next page. You may find it useful to bookmark this page so you have ready access to the complete list of these principles.

Turn the page to see all 25 Life Improvement Principles!

Simple! 25 Life Improvement Principles

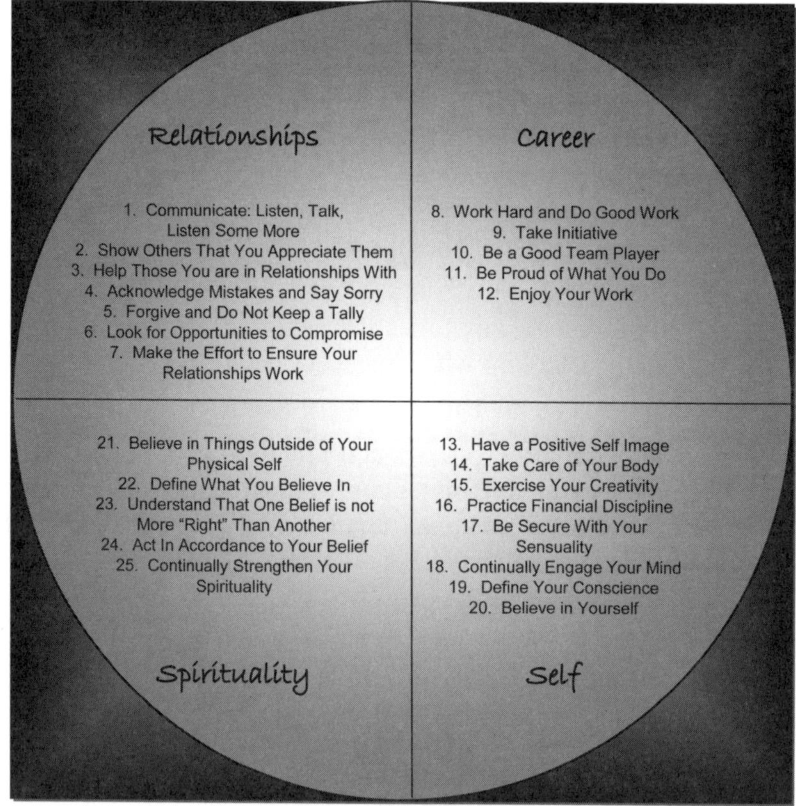

"Look at your results for your lowest, or two lowest scoring Life Aspects and then refer to the corresponding Life Principles. For example, if your career Life Aspect needs the most improvement, look at the principles in the career section. Go down the list of the five principles and ask yourself if you successfully meet these principles in your current job. If not, identify those that are not met, and write these down. Do this exercise for each Life Aspect that needs improvement," instructs Fixity Fox as Pouting Pig begins to review the Life Principles.

After Pouting Pig has completed writing down some of the Life Improvement Principles, Fixity Fox continues, "Now, refer to Section 6 of your survey results and let's determine what statements from your survey need improving. Begin with the statements that are in the category 'Needs Immediate Improvement,' or your first listed category. Review the statements (remember that the lowest scoring statements are presented first) and select a few to write down to improve."

Pouting Pig follows Fixity Fox's instructions. After some time has passed, Fixity Fox asks, "So what does your list look like?"

"I have ten items on my list! Is that good or bad?"

"Remember what I said earlier: don't think of your results as either good or bad. However, in terms of improvement actions, ten items will probably be a lot to work on at one time, so we need to make the list more manageable. How do you think we can do this?"

Pouting Pig thinks for a moment and then gets so excited that he trips over a tree root as he springs up with the answer, "PRIORITIZE!" He yells as he falls into the dirt. "WE HAVE TO PRIORITIZE!"

"Ahhh! What an apt pupil you are!" Fixity Fox responds, sharing in Pouting Pig's excitement. "You are correct. We must prioritize your list."

Activity 2: Prioritize Your Items

"Look at your list of items," Fixity Fox instructs. "I suggest that we prioritize the items from 1-3, with 1 being the highest priority. Then determine what criteria you'll use to prioritize your items. Here are a couple of different ways to prioritize your items:

Example 1

Priority	Description
1	▪ Easy/quick to improve
2	▪ A bit more effort/longer to improve
3	▪ Possibly not able to improve/longer term item

Example 2

Priority	Description
1	▪ Directly related to Purpose Statement
2	▪ Somewhat related to Purpose Statement
3	▪ Not related to Purpose Statement

"You may decide that items you're best able to improve in the near-term, or with less effort should receive a 1. In consultant-speak, we refer to these types of items as 'low hanging fruit,' Or, you may decide to assign a 1 to those items that relate directly to your Purpose Statement. For items that may take a bit longer to improve, or are only somewhat related to your Purpose Statement, you may decide to assign a 2. Lastly, you may decide to assign a 3 to the items you feel you may not be able to improve, or that are not related to your Purpose Statement. Now, go ahead and assign priorities to the items on your list."

Pouting Pig begins assigning priorities while Fixity Fox does the same for his items.

Activity 3: Identify Improvement Actions and Create Your Plan

"I'm done," says Pouting Pig after he has assigned his priorities.

"Good. Now that you have your items prioritized, identify one of your high priority items, and tell me what action items you can think of to improve it."

Pouting Pig looks at his list and says, "Based on one of the Life Improvement Principles, to improve my relationships, I need to help those I am in relationships with."

"Good, what relationships do you need to improve?"

"I guess the ones with my sister and brother since we always fight."

"Okay, name some action items you can take to improve these relationships."

"My brother hunts for truffles. I could help him sniff them out," suggests Pouting Pig.

"Good example!" Fixity Fox exclaims. "To help you identify additional action items you can perform for each Life Aspect, I created some examples for you." Fixity Fox hands Pouting Pig the following lists of activities.

Life Aspect—Relationships

Principle	Actions
Principle #1: Communicate: Listen, Talk, Listen Some More	▪ Identify which relationships need improved communication. ▪ Identify specific actions you can take to improve the communication. ▪ Carve out specific times (e.g., in the evening after work) to communicate.
Principle #2: Show Others That You Appreciate Them	▪ Identify who in your life you appreciate. ▪ Perform simple gestures to show them that you appreciate them.
Principle #3: Help Those You are in Relationships With	▪ Identify those you have relationships with, that could need help that you can provide. ▪ Volunteer to provide your help—this includes simple tasks, or complex tasks.
Principle #4: Acknowledge Your Mistakes and Learn to Say Sorry	▪ Identify where you made mistakes, or treated someone badly. ▪ Approach the individual and apologize for the past mistakes. ▪ Practice acknowledging your mistakes as you make them: you don't have to wait until later!
Principle #5: Forgive and Do Not Keep a Running Tally	▪ Identify someone who made a mistake or did you wrong—someone you have not forgiven. ▪ Forgive that person, and if the person continues to make the mistakes, change the nature of the relationship.
Principle #6: Look for Opportunities to Compromise	▪ Identify opportunities to value the other person, instead of "having your way." ▪ Identify a situation where you are currently "sticking to your guns" and think of a way you could compromise. Tell the other person of your proposed compromise.
Principle #7: Make the Effort to Ensure Your Relationships Work	▪ Evaluate the actions you have taken relative to Principles 1—6. ▪ What worked? What did not? ▪ Keep practicing the things that worked; find new approaches to those that did not.

Life Aspect—Career

Principle	Actions
Principle #8: Work Hard and Do Good Work	■ Identify someone at your job who works hard. ■ Compare your work effort to the hard worker and honestly asses your level of effort at your job. Do you work hard or not? ■ If not, identify actions you can take to work harder, e.g.: – Emulate the hard worker at your job. – Arrive at work earlier. – Reduce the amount of non-work activities you perform at work. ■ Identify someone at your job who does quality work. ■ Compare the quality of your work, and honestly assess the quality of your work. Is it good or not? ■ If not, identify actions you can take to improve the quality, e.g.: – Identify and attend training to improve your skills. – Ask for help from the co-worker who does quality work.
Principle #9: Take Initiative	■ Do a project at your job that you were not asked to do. ■ Brainstorm a list of ideas to improve your work environment. Develop one or two of them and volunteer to implement them.
Principle #10: Be a Good Team Player	■ Volunteer to help an employee who needs assistance. ■ Pick up a co-worker's slack. ■ Appreciate coworkers for their contributions.
Principle #11: Be Proud of What You Do	■ Pay close attention to all aspects of your job: no detail is too small to matter! ■ Don't belittle your job or organization to others.
Principle #12: Enjoy Your Work	■ Identify tasks at your job that you enjoy doing—and find ways to do these tasks more often. ■ If you can't enjoy **anything** in your job—look for another job!

Life Aspect—Self

Principle	Actions
Principle #13 Have a Positive Self Image	▪ Write down a list of things you like about yourself. Do you have less than 5 items on your list? ▪ Write down a list of things you don't like about yourself. Which list is larger? ▪ Identify actions you can take to move "don't likes" to the "likes" list.
Principle #14 Take Care of Your Body	▪ Identity ways in which you are currently not taking care of your body (e.g., smoking, eating too much, using harmful substances). ▪ Identify actions to stop those harmful activities. (Remember, I told you this was simple stuff—it's not rocket science!) ▪ Take up a sport (e.g., go on Craigslist.com and identify some tennis lessons).
Principle #15 Exercise Your Creativity	▪ Identify creative things that interest you (drawing, singing, playing a musical instrument, etc.). ▪ Identify actions you can take to begin doing one of these creative activities.
Principle #16 Practice Financial Discipline	▪ Identify how much money you bring in each month and itemize your monthly expenses. Subtract expenses from income to determine your "net income." ▪ Identify ways to increase your net income by: – Increasing your pay (e.g., part-time job, new job). – Decreasing your expenses (eliminate "nice to have" items).
Principle #17 Be Secure With Your Sensuality	▪ Seek professional help if you have experienced sexual violence or abuse. ▪ Make sure you've addressed Principles 13 and 14!
Principle #18 Continually Engage Your Mind	▪ Read books and newspapers. ▪ Do crosswords puzzles and mind teasers. ▪ Talk with others about interesting topics. ▪ Take courses at a local college or learning center.
Principle #19: Define Your Conscience and Act Accordingly	▪ Define right and wrong—then do the right things; don't do the wrong things! ▪ Volunteer to help others (e.g., contact a local volunteer agency; go to Craigslist.com to the volunteer section).
Principle #20: Believe in Yourself	▪ Stop doubting yourself. ▪ Set a goal and achieve it.

Life Aspect—Spirituality

Principle	Actions
Principle #21: Believe in Things Outside of Your Physical Self	▪ Identify things you believe in that are outside of you and your control. ▪ Identify things you believe in that you cannot see or hear.
Principle #22: Define What You Believe In	▪ Based on what you identified in Principle #21, write down your beliefs. ▪ Include what you feel is "right," and what's "wrong." ▪ Identify what you feel your role in this world is.
Principle #23: Understand That One Belief is not More "Right" Than Another	▪ Identify beliefs counter to yours. ▪ Identify why the other beliefs are different than yours. ▪ Learn to accept the fact that others have beliefs just as strong as yours, even though they may be different.
Principle #24: Act In Accordance to Your Belief	▪ Honestly identify areas where you do not practice what you preach. ▪ List specific actions you can take that are right (as defined in Principle #22). ▪ List specific actions you should stop doing/or not do because they are "wrong" (as defined in Principle #22).
Principle #25: Continually Strengthen Your Spirituality	▪ Read material related to your beliefs regularly. ▪ Read material **not** related to your beliefs. ▪ Meet regularly with others that share your beliefs (e.g., attend church, bible-study, have informal meetings, etc.). ▪ Practice Principle #24 every day!

After Pouting Pig has looked over the lists, Fixity Fox continues, "Once you have identified the action items you want to accomplish, you document them on your ***Life Improvement Action Plan***. And for those really anal about things—"

"What does anal mean?" Pouting Pig interrupts.

"Scratch that," laughs Fox. "For those who really want to be thorough, your action plan can capture multiple pieces of information, as shown by this example."

Example Action Plan

Life Aspect	Action Items	Status
Relationships	▪ Designate time each day to talk to my children about their day.	▪ In progress.
	▪ Help my wife by picking up the children from soccer practice every other Saturday.	▪ Starting next week.
Spirituality	▪ Begin attending weekly church services with the entire family.	▪ Beginning next Sunday.
	▪ Begin going to weekly bible study.	▪ Find out when classes are.

<u>Activity 4: Put the Plan Into Action!</u>

"Now the fun begins," says Fixity Fox. "You now have to implement your plan."

"How do I do that?" Pouting Pig asks.

"Simply put, you start doing what you said you should do! Let your action plan be your to-do list. Weave your action plan items into your every day routine. A key characteristic of your action items is to make them regularly occurring actions, versus one-time only actions. And your plan is a living document, which means that you can always change it to suit your needs and time commitments."

"Let's look at how all of the information I gave you fits together—by looking at what I wrote for myself while you were working on your items," says Fixity Fox.

Fixity Fox' Own Life Improvement Plan Information

What's Important to Me (*Results Section 1*):	Career—92% Relationships—84%
What I Need to Improve (*Results Sections 5 & 6*):	Career—57% (Needs Immediate Improvement) ▪ Being fulfilled with the job I perform. (Priority 1) ▪ Doing what I'm best suited to do. (Priority 1) Relationships—70% (Needs Some Improvement) ▪ Number of fulfilling relationships I have. (Priority 1) ▪ Amount of time I spend on relationships. (Priority 2) Spirituality—85% (Almost There) ▪ Have a sense of purpose that extends beyond myself. (Priority 1)
My Purpose Statement (*Based on information above*):	My purpose in life is to engage in career-related endeavors that then give me the means to help others. My purpose is to also have fulfilling relationships that benefit myself and positively affect others.

Action Plan

Life Aspect	Action Items	Status
Career	▪ Begin doing something more satisfying with my career, like writing a book that helps others.	▪ By the end of the summer.
Career, Spirituality	▪ To give my life purpose beyond myself, determine how to financially help the less fortunate based on the work I do.	▪ By the end of the summer.
Relationships	▪ Form fulfilling relationships; begin thinking about starting a family. ▪ Begin to spend more time with friends and family.	▪ Within the year. ▪ ASAP.

"Wow!" Pouting Pig says after looking at Fixity Fox's information. "Now I see how it all fits together. Will you help me Fixity—to make sure I do my action items?"

"Of course. In fact, having someone help you with your action plan is, as we consultants say, a Best Practice. And as your helper, I will help ensure that you're doing what you said you would do, and once a week, you will report to me on your progress."

"Have you picked anyone to help you with your action plan?" Pouting Pig asks.

"Not yet."

"Then you can report to me on your progress as well."

"Wow, I'll have my own Life Improvement Consultant!" jokes Fixity Fox. "I feel important!"

"Don't get too excited—wait until you get my bill. And if you don't pay, I'll sic Confident Cat on you!"

"You're getting a little too comfortable there Pig," replies Fixity Fox as he playfully snaps one of Pouting Pig's overall straps. "Mess with me, and I just might develop a taste for barbeque ribs—I've got a whole mess of that *Fox's Finger Licking Fire* I need to use!"

"Barbeque ribs—what's that?" asks Pouting Pig.

"Scratch that!" laughs Fixity Fox, and with that, the two animals began a lifelong friendship.

Fixity Fox's Action Plan Guidelines

- Identify the Life Aspects and survey statements related to your Purpose Statement that you want to improve.
- Pick a manageable number of items to improve by prioritizing.
- Write down very concrete action items with specific time-frames.
- Weave your action items into your normal routine.
- Identify action items that can be done more than just once.
- Identify someone to assist you with your progress.
- Do what you said you would do!

Reader Reflection:

Have you created improvement plans before? Did they work? If not, why not? In my consulting with businesses, I have found that organizational improvement plans fail to work when they are too complex and contain too many items. This makes the plan seem daunting, time consuming, and difficult to maintain. Plus, employees often state that they're too busy with their normal jobs to take on added activities. These same issues surface with individuals in their personal lives. Don't we already have packed schedules? How are we going to add yet more activities?

The key is simplicity. If you really want a simple improvement plan, prioritize your list and start by developing your plan with only **one** item—the highest prioritized item. And then accomplish that one item before adding another one or two items. Unless you have a serious situation, there's no rush to improve everything all at once!

Have you noticed how you are more motivated to do something if you know you have to report progress to someone? **Assignment 1:** I strongly advocate that you identify someone to assist you in meeting your goals. Think of who this person will be. Why did you select this person? And don't feel bad about needing help. Look at successful athletes—they all have a trainer, a coach or teammates to help them. Rarely are they successful without the help of someone else urging them on, or giving them advice and pointers. So, why should you go it alone?

Assignment 2: Lastly, incorporate some of the simple improvement activities into your normal routine. Notice how we always find time in our lives to do the things that we just "have" to do? You brush your teeth every day don't you? Then how hard could it be to do one or two simple improvement items on a regular basis?

Chapter 9: Where Are They Now?

We created a plan based on what we needed to improve.
We made a change, and guess what: it didn't hurt us!
We're no longer pouting; instead we're happy,
Because we ended up finding our purpose!

Each animal involved in the story learned something from their meetings with Fixity Fox and Pouting Pig. Each one took the Life Improvement Survey and created a short and long-term action plan. The results? Ten years after their initial meeting, here's an update:

- ***Fixity Fox***: He realized he needed to make major changes in terms of his relationships and his career. After receiving additional guidance from Lovable Lab, he met someone (she's a real Fox!) and got married. He began a new career by becoming a life improvement coach, moved to the big city, and now has his own afternoon television talk show. His long-term goal is to establish his own movie studio—*21st Century Fox*. He regularly donates a percentage of his earnings to the KFC (Kindness For Chickens) Foundation established by Conscience Cat.

- ***Pouting Pig:*** Pouting Pig, now called Purposeful Pig, liked learning new words from Fixity Fox so much, that not long after their initial meeting, he entered and won the All-County Spelling Bee. Purposeful Pig also began spending time with Conscience Cat and became interested in politics. He ended up going to college (Pig Penn State) where he studied Piglitical science, and is currently a lawyer, and has a goal of becoming a politician so he can reduce pork-barrel spending.

- ***Lovable Lab:*** Lovable Lab married Leonard the Lab, and they now have four children. Encouraged by her success in helping Fixity Fox with his relationships, she decided to help others, and co-wrote a book with Creative Cat called *Dogs are from Pluto, Cats are From Neptune*, describing how to make difficult relationships work.

- ***Hardworking Horses:*** The husband and wife team retired from field work and stayed at home for awhile, but they got bored. So, they decided to own their own business, and with the help of Cash Cat, they bought and now manage a horse racing track and equestrian center. (The Show Horses work for them!)

- Creative Cat: In addition to writing the book with Lovable Lab, Creative Cat became a famous painter. She studied the work of Andy Warthog and is best known for her painting Cat Food Cans.

- ***Confident Cat:*** He moved away from the farm and became a famous weightlifter, stared in a number of very popular action movies, and is now running for the governor of Catifornia. Asked if he'll ever go back to the farm, he replied, "I'll be back!"

- ***Conscience Cat:*** Because of her numerous protests, she spent some time in and out of the pen. She has meowed out a bit and currently lives on a commune on Catalina Island, where she is heading-up a political movement formed to defeat her brother's campaign for governor.

- ***Coquette Cat:*** She met a T.V. producer who came to the farm to film an episode of *The Simple Life*, got bitten by the acting bug, and she is currently the sexy lead actress in the hit television show *Desperate Housepets*.

- ***Cerebral Cat:*** He studied math and physics and wrote a scientific paper proving that it's an urban myth that cats have nine lives (they actually have 7.8 lives).

- ***Cash Cat:*** Cash Cat is busy helping to run the horse track with the Hardworking Horses. He is also Confident Cat's Campaign Manager for Governor and Coquette Cat's talent agent. But all is not purrfect: he currently has a beef with Cash Cow, who is suing him for mismanagement of funds.

- ***Omniscient Owl:*** Shortly after the conversation with Fixity Fox and Pouting Pig, she went on a pilgrimage to see the *Dalai Llama* and came back to the farm with deeper spirituality. Later, she met and married *Jerry Owlwell*, and they now operate a mega-church and a television ministry.

Author's Epilogue

I'm not sure if you guessed it or not, but the character of Fixity Fox is based loosely on me. For years, many around me felt that my main focus in life was on my job, and that I didn't spend as much time as I should on relationships and those around me.

I've had the idea for this book since the late 1990s, but it took a couple of things in my life to happen for me to finally write and finish the book. Two people (the women to whom I dedicated the book) showed me what was really important in life. The first woman, whom I dated years ago, died earlier this year, and I went to her funeral, where many of her friends and co-workers spoke and praised her. It was clear based on their comments that she had great relationships and did things that helped others. While sitting in the church pew, I broke down and cried for the first time in almost 25 years, as I realized how good a person she was. And if you had asked her when she was alive about her purpose, she would not have stated that she had a grand purpose—and that's one of the points I wish to make with this book—you don't need a grand purpose to lead a satisfying life and to touch many around you with your character and deeds.

The second woman, who entered my life in the last couple of years, and helped me with the book, used to get perturbed a bit when I would joke that she was Pouting Pig and I was her Fixity Fox—brought into her life to fix her "problems." So, wasn't it ironic that, much like Fixity Fox, I realized, that based on her attitude about life and the people around us, she was better off than I was in many areas.

When I took the Life Improvement survey I was a Hardworking Horse. Yes, my career was important to me, but it wasn't all that satisfying. I learned that I got satisfaction from helping others—but this is where I needed to improve. I also needed improvement in the relationships Life Aspect. As a result of my assessment, I wrote the following Purpose Statement (which should look familiar):

My purpose in life is to engage in career-related endeavors that then give me the means to help others. My purpose is to also have fulfilling relationships that benefit myself and positively affect others.

It's not a grand purpose statement—it's pretty simple. And for the first part of the statement, one way I can accomplish this is financially. Therefore, I plan to donate 10% of the profits from this book, and others I write in the future, to charity.

For the second part of the statement, I plan to devote more time to the people in my life. I also plan to settle down and start a loving family—but first I've got to find someone… now, what was that website that Fixity Fox bookmarked?

- Harold Kerr

About The Author

Harold Kerr, M.B.A., is a professional management consultant who has worked for companies such as Arthur Andersen LLP, MCI, Verizon, Nortel and Booz Allen Hamilton. He currently has his own management consulting company—The Kerr Company LLC, with an objective of *Helping Clients Implement Results*®.

In his work, Harold assists organizations in the areas of corporate strategy, organizational development, business process reengineering, change management, and information technology. Harold also has extensive experience in working with groups of employees during the conduct of his work. He has conducted employee satisfaction surveys, personnel assessments, 360 degree feedback sessions, and he has a wealth of experience organizing and facilitating employee focus group sessions.

It is from these diverse experiences working with organizations and their employees, that Harold obtained his insight pertinent to writing a self-help book for individuals. Harold feels that many problems faced by organizations and their employees, and the approaches to fix them, are transferable to assisting individuals.

Harold has his M.B.A. from The George Washington University in Washington D.C., with a concentration in Organizational Development.

Harold can be reached at: Haroldkerr@thekerrcompany.com and at: http://www.thekerrcompany.com.

Acknowledgements

I would like to thank:

1. Krystalle Campo, who provided a wealth of material for the book.
2. Doris Maultsby, my sister, who I forced to keep reading all my drafts.
3. Michael Lewis, of On Message Communications, who gave valuable feedback on the book.
4. Tracey Williams and Mirza Donegan, who read drafts of the book.
5. Allen Mueller and Maxie Maultsby, who went the extra mile and provided feedback on the survey.
6. Eric Paulson, from Viking Development, who developed the web survey.
7. Jay Mazhar, for his illustrations.
8. Lisa J. Voss, the Editor, who pointed out that I needed to tie up loose ends.
9. Gabrielle Faulcon, who jumped in, rolled up her sleeves and helped out.
10. Donny Wyatt, the future CIO for his assistance.
11. All of the people (many from Craigslist.com) that took the test survey, read the draft book and took the reader survey.
12. Taman31, whom I've never met, but called me each morning at 5:00 a.m. so I could work on the book.
13. To Craigslist.com—which made the process of self-publishing and marketing much easier.

BOOK ORDERING INSTRUCTIONS

In addition to selected online book sites, books can be ordered a bit cheaper directly from the publisher at the following website:

http://www.poutorpurpose.com.

Additionally, discounts will be given for purchases of multiple books. The book makes a perfect gift for organized groups of adults, book clubs, or youth organizations.
Get your group together, take the Pout or Purpose Survey, and see what a bunch of animals you are!

The publisher can be contacted at the following address:

K.C. Fox Publishing
P.O. Box 5446
Takoma Park, Maryland 20913
An All-American City!

Email: publisher@kcfoxpublishing.com